THE SANE

VOLUME XI

BY: TODD ANDREW ROHRER

iUniverse, Inc.
New York Bloomington

THE SANE
SUBTITLE

iUniverse books may be ordered through booksellers or by contacting:

iUniverse
1663 Liberty Drive
Bloomington, IN 47403
www.iuniverse.com
1-800-Authors (1-800-288-4677)

ISBN: 978-1-4401-9665-2 (pbk)
ISBN: 978-1-4401-9666-9 (ebook)

Printed in the United States of America

iUniverse rev. date:12/01/09

There are many books you are perhaps capable of understanding
but this is not one of them.

"for I have sworn upon the altar of god eternal hostility against every form of tyranny over the mind of man." –*Thomas Jefferson to Benjamin Rush, 23 Sept. 1800*

Greetings. Dawn your snorkel. Tyranny over the mind relates to changing a subjects mind into a state that is pleasing to a tyrant. A tyrant is a person or group of people who seek control and employ methods to retain control. The trend of a tyrant is to create a reward system. The tyrant's subjects who conform to its control desires are rewarded and the subjects that resist the control desires are punished. This control method is similar to a rat in a cage that gets a food reward for pushing the right button and does not get a food reward if it pushes the wrong button.

The tyrant uses elementary punishment reward aspects to slowly gain control over the subjects mind. The most important goal of a tyrant is to disguise the mental control techniques it wishes to employ over the subject with rewards that appear to be freedom. This is along the lines of suggesting "If you stay in line you will not be punished so that means you will be free." This is simply a control method in relation to, "If you jump through the hoop you will be free" when in reality jumping through the hoop only leads to the subject becoming more controlled by the tyrant.

The tyrant uses food as a background control mechanism because food is too obvious to use as an upfront control mechanism so the tyrant uses money as an upfront control mechanism. The logic is, without money one has no food so the money is simply a method to disguise the fact that food is the bottom line control mechanism. So the suggestion is "If you jump through the hoops you get the chance for lots of money." Then the subject will automatically understand they will have plenty of food if they have plenty of money. This is elementary carrot and stick tactics. There are no subjects who go to school to get education, they go to school for the opportunity to make money and that means the opportunity to get food.

This money opportunity creates an urgency. On one hand get educated and on the other hand get as educated as much as possible. The logic being the more education the more money and thus the easier it will be to afford food. The subject has it in their mind if they

1

have lots of food, certainly life will be easy so the more education they get the more money potential they will have and thus the more food they will have, and thus the easier their life will be.

The tyrant knows food is the key to keeping the subject jumping through hoops just like a scientist knows food is the key to keep that rat jumping through the hoops. This is a form of blackmail or extortion because it suggests if the subject does not jump through the hoops they will not have food and they will in turn die.

No subject wants to die so they tyrant is careful to ensure it has control over the food. Once the tyrant controls the food the rats will do as the tyrant suggests because they know the tyrant has the food. Once the food is controlled by the tyrant everything else falls in line in relation to controlling the subjects.

The easiest way for the tyrant to control the food supplies is for the tyrant to create organizations that grow the food. Once the organizations of subjects that grow the food are achieved then the tyrant can create control structures and laws so that too much food is never grown. The logic being the more food there is the more difficult it is for the tyrant to control his subjects. The main goal of the tyrant is to ensure his subjects rely on him for survival so the tyrant becomes the hand that feeds them so then the subjects are in servitude to the tyrant. As long as the tyrant controls the food supply he will have control over the subjects.

The tyrant cannot hold food over the subjects that grow the food so he has to use money as a bait to manipulate the ones who grow the food. The logic of the subjects who grow the food is "If the tyrant will not buy my food then I will not have money to grow food." The tyrant uses that leverage in order to convince the food grower subjects to only grow certain amounts of food and certain kinds of food. This creates an artificial supply and demand and in that system is where the tyrant's power is achieved over the food growers.

Food itself is the main control aspect used by the tyrant and so it is important for the subject of the tyrant to be hungry. So hunger itself is the deeper control mechanism. A hungry subject will jump happily through burning hoops. Because of this it is important for the tyrant to make sure the majority of his subjects cannot readily grow their own food or raise their own food. As the ability of the subjects to supply their own food increases the power of the tyrant decreases. Because of this threat to the tyrant the tyrant must keep the subjects congregated.

The ideal situation is to never teach any form of agriculture in the basic education system. The less the tyrants subjects know about agriculture the better. The tyrant does not want his subjects to get any crazy ideas like they can supply their own food. As long as the majority of the subjects do not grow their own food, the majority of the subjects will not think for their self. The best way for a tyrant to ensure this is to create regulations or laws that make sure the majority of his subjects will never be able to grow and supply their own food needs. The best way to achieve that is to cram all the subjects together and then pass regulations suggesting one cannot grow or raise food in such close proximity to other subjects for health reasons for example.

No chickens in city limits because certainly the chickens will kill everyone if they get loose. The tyrant will use any of his subjects to convince the majority this is a proper law. The tyrant will use 'experts" in the medical field to convince the majority subjects, growing food is in fact bad. As long as the majority subjects believe growing food is bad for one's health they will never reach a point of growing their own food and so the tyrant will always control the food supply.

Once the possibility of the majority of the tyrants subjects to grow food is eliminated the tyrant's absolute power is achieved. The tyrant has so many "experts" with certain titles in front of their name that it is nearly impossible for the tyrant to not have a convincing argument to thrust upon his subjects at any given time to steer them towards his aims. If the tyrant can keep everyone in a little box in the city then he can always use his medical experts to explain why his subjects cannot grow their own food and so he can never lose his control over the food supply.

The logic is for the tyrant to keep everyone packed tightly and then if anyone tries to grow their own food then the tyrant will suggest there simply is not enough room and there are health risks and certainly it is dangerous to grow your own food in such a tightly packed sardine can. Once the food supply is controlled by the tyrant then the organization that supplies the food is under the tyrants hand as well. All of the food supplied by the organization must then be regulated by the tyrant and thus the tyrant gets a cut of the action.

If a subject is growing their own food the tyrant does not get a cut of the action. This is why there will never be a class that teaches agriculture in the basic education system. The education system teaches one how to work within the tyrants system or within the rules created by the tyrant. No education, no money and thus no food. In fact the tyrant is so clever at demonizing growing your own food his own subjects will mock anyone who is a farmer, as if growing your own food is evil, as if supplying your own food needs is illegal, or one is stupid to supply their own food needs. This mindset is what keeps the tyrant in absolute control. Every single profession has to do with getting enough food to keep living. Having a roof over your head is secondary to having enough food. Everything is secondary to having enough food and the tyrant controls the food, and that includes water and salt supplies, so the tyrant is in absolute control over everything. - 4:09:19 PM

9/29/2009 8:48:02 AM-
Left brain = Sequential thoughts
Right Brain = Random Access Thoughts
Written language is sequential based in relation to ABC's are in sequential order and words spelled with letters in proper sequential order.
Math is also sequential in relation to 123. Counting is sequential.

After years of this education one goes into an extreme left brain state of mind and this affects the Hypothalamus aspect of the brain and increases fear. Hypothalamus is the aspect of the brain that tells one when to fight or flight/run. When this aspect of the brain is not functioning properly due to the mind being conditioned into extreme left brain from the education one might be afraid of intangible things, such a words or even the dark.

In order to break this extreme left brain state of mind fear conditioning must be applied.

This means ones fear of things like words and certain pictures and anything one does not like such as certain music, must be embraced

4

or faced in order to shock the hypothalamus back into working order. The most harsh but quickest way to do this is to face ones fear of perceived death. One example would be to watch a very scary movie then turn out the lights while one is alone and that hypothalamus will tell one to run for the lights but they must not do that, so that is fear conditioning. In some cases going to a very spooky location alone and sitting and fighting the urge to run for help is another method.

The education which is sequential based is the root of problems and that means we are mentally harming children because there is no fear or emotional conditioning in the schools.

The sequential left brain state of mind education does not alter the brain physiologically but alters the mind to the left, and in turn all of the little parts of the brain do not send proper signals.

These are some patterns I write about in the 9th and 10th book and its important because religion itself understood what the written language was doing to peoples mind and they tried to explain it so the ancient texts are perhaps not about supernatural they are in fact perhaps the first psychology/neurology texts.

5:19:01 PM – An email to someone about something.

[Genesis 3:6 And when the woman saw that the tree was good for food, and that it was pleasant to the eyes, and a tree to be desired to make one wise,]
So this line explains written language looks pleasing to the eyes referring to characters, letters and it is thought to make one wise, and of course the sane assume the education makes one wise.

After one gets the education these ancient texts describe symptoms. [Genesis 3:14 And the LORD God said unto the serpent, Because thou hast done this, thou art cursed above all cattle, and above every beast of the field; upon thy belly shalt thou go, and dust shalt thou eat all the days of thy life:]
And cursed is a good way to say extreme left brain state because one is mentally unsound and one symptom is they are slothful, sequential thoughts as opposed to right brain random access thoughts, and physically orientated instead of cerebrally orientated.

And the strong symptom fear aspect is explained clearly here.

[2 Timothy 1:7 For God hath not given us the spirit of fear; but of power, and of love, and of a sound mind.]

So the hypothalamus is altered and sending wrong signals so the sane fear words and pictures and ghosts and all of these things and this line says fear is a symptom of an unsound mind and an unsound mind is a mind that gets this education and does not apply the remedy and the remedy is simply stated here.
[Genesis 15:1 After these things the word of the LORD came unto Abram in a vision, saying, Fear not, Abram: I am thy shield, and thy exceeding great reward.]

So the hypothalamus creates this extreme fear and that is in line with the Amygdala which keeps memories of fear and also is relative to emotions. So then there are the patterns relative to this fear not remedy, if one has to much fear the remedy would be fear not.
Abraham demonstrated this fear not remedy using the Abraham and Isaac story. Abraham held a knife over Isaac and Isaac did not run so he faced his fear of death so he applied fear not or Isaac submitted to perceived fear.

Jesus tried to explain it also:
[Luke 17:33 ..; and whosoever shall lose his life shall preserve it.]
So Isaac did not run when the knife was over him, so he lost, let go of his life mentally and he preserved it which means reverted back to sound state of mind which is 50/50 left and right brain.
Then Mohammed came along and tried to reduce the fear not comment to one word which is submit. And so Isaac did not run when the knife was over mind so he submitted to his fear of death. Socrates said no true philosopher fears death.
A Buddhist method is go sit in a cemetery at night until you feel better.
      Society as a whole continues to condition children into this state of mind and so Jesus said Suffer the children and Socrates was told to drink the hemlock because he was corrupting the minds of the youth. So if the adults continue to mentally condition the children into this state of mind and are not even aware of it then they know

not what they do. Insanity is a person who knows not what they do. A person possessed is also a person who knows not what they do.

Nature itself will not tolerate a creature that is unviable or out of harmony and in this mental state. So the sane are unsound mentally in the left brain state and they also continue to condition the next generation into this unsound mental state.

So I do not detect any way there is to stop it and that is what this comment means.

[Genesis 3:14 And the LORD God said unto the serpent,]

I do not detect supernatural but I also do not detect any of the sane are going to commit mental suicide to wake up which is what this is [Luke 17:33 ..; and whosoever shall lose his life shall preserve it.]

So what I think I am engaged in my 11th book since the accident 11 months ago is what is known as infinite vanity.
[1 John 2:18 Little children, it is the last time: and as ye have heard that antichrist shall come, even now are there many antichrists; whereby we know that it is the last time.]

Did I wake up to a world full of mentally unsound people or did I wake up to a world full of demon possessed people because I do not see a difference in the two any longer.
END

9/30/2009 1:44:40 AM – I have spoken with people who woke up as the result of meditating while on psychotropic drugs and I have spoken with people who woke up as the result of near death experiences caused by trauma such as strokes or heart attacks and then I have spoken to those who woke up as a result of using various meditation techniques.

There are ones who wake up as the result of a failed suicide. They tend to have more urgency in their ways. It is not relative to them being better it is more relative to them being driven by vengeance because they went was a known as the full measure. When a person wakes up as the result of failed suicide attempt and then understands the only reason they were suicidal is because of the "education" they got as a child they are unable to ever forgive those who educated them and they tend to get slaughtered by the sane because they only have one thing in their eyes and that is retribution or a reckoning, and that motivation is what the concept judgment day is all about. - 1:55:43 AM

6:33:27 AM – The reality about Gandhi is that he did not oppose the British as much as he opposed the carpetbaggers, and they are the sane. They are the ones conditioned by written education who have not applied the remedy, and they are the serpent, and they number like the grains of sand in the sea, and they are cursed, and they are the taskmasters, and they are tyrants, and they are the adversaries, and they are the beast.

9:34:32 AM – Peace is an option our species no longer has. The militant state of mind the species as a whole has is a direct result of the sequential left brain conditioning caused by written education and math. It is not our species is militant because our species naturally is militant, it is our species is militant because that is the nature of the mind when it is unsound as a result of the education.

In the extreme left brain state one is left in after the education because the remedy is never suggested or applied, one only see's things as parts and seeing as parts is a left brain trait. This seeing thing's as parts ensures violence and this violent tendency is proof nature itself will not tolerate mutations physiologically or mentally. The ones who do apply the remedy are prone to be militant against ones who have not applied the remedy for the sake of the species and in turn the ones who have not applied the remedy become militant against the ones who have applied the remedy and their belief is, it is for the sake of the species.

The whole concept of peace is no longer possible because peace itself is no longer possible because nature will in its own way pit the species against itself to get rid of an unsound or unviable species. It has nothing to do with morality because that is a narrow minded view of the situation. Anything that is out of harmony is doomed to collapse. A mind built on sand, the left brain mental state, will collapse just as a species built on sand, vast majority is educated and thus in the left brain mental state, will collapse.

The human species is a part of an ecological system and the ecological system itself has determined the human species is intolerable. The militant aspect of our species is in the homes, in the neighborhoods, in the cities, in the states and in the countries. Countries are at war with each other. This has nothing to do with people not being proper this has to do with the species continuing to condition people with the education and having no idea they are conditioning people into an unsound state of mind and so the species itself is killing itself on one hand, and nature is also making sure the species kills itself off on the other hand. This perhaps has nothing to do with religion this has to do with basic ecological reality. A species with an unsound mind is not viable and thus dies off.

[Genesis 13:13 But the men of Sodom were wicked and sinners before the LORD exceedingly.]

Wicked and sin is suggesting unsound state of mind in contrast to the Lords. In this case it is Abraham and the tribes or the ones who applied the remedy fear not after the written language education or ones who never got said conditioning.

Abraham understood one thing very clearly. He had to totally wipe out this new form of creature he called man and the reason is because of what we have now. There are ones even today who are still fighting against the creature called man. Even when man has taken over everything; has thousands of cities of Sodom and continues to educate the next generation and not apply the remedy, and thus leave the children in an unsound state of mind and thus ensure the annihilation of the species from within.

Even now this creature called man is conditioning their children and then they complain why their child has emotional problems and then they tell that child to go get a construction job and make something of your life.

[Genesis 11:5 And the LORD came down to see the city and the tower, which the children of men builded.]

So these creatures called men mentally ruin their children with this education because they do not have the mental capacity to understand its ill effects on the mind and then they blame the children for not being wise enough.

There was only one solution to the problem, kill them all without mercy or questions.

[Genesis 19:24 Then the LORD rained upon Sodom and upon Gomorrah brimstone and fire from the LORD out of heaven;
Genesis 19:25 And he overthrew those cities, and all the plain, and all the inhabitants of the cities, and that which grew upon the ground.]

Abraham killed all the inhabitants of the cities because they were too far gone. But the reason he never had a chance is because the written language was all over the world by this time. Socrates woke up around this time and he tried to warn of the dangers of this written language and he was killed. Socrates was killed for corrupting the mind of the youth, he was telling the youth there was some problems with this man made invention called written language, demotic, and math. Buddha woke up about this time and he tried to warn of the dangers in his area of the world. It was too late because written language was a drug that was far too pleasing.

Even today there are billions of people who cannot grasp that twelve years of hardcore sequential conditioning which is what written language and math is could possibly hinder or unbalance the mind.

These beings are not even in the realms of sanity any longer because they cannot even grasp obvious cause and effect relationships. They will try to make a case that the abc's are not in sequential order. They will try to make a case that making sure the letters in a word, which is spelling, is not sequence relative. They will make the case the memorizing numbers from smaller to larger is not sequence relative. They can no longer even grasp obvious patterns because their right brain, pattern detector, is so veiled they no longer have the ability to detect any patterns at all.

The deeper reality is they do not want to face the fact they were robbed of their mind and thus their life by about the age of ten. The tree of knowledge was fatal to the species and the problems they are experiencing are simply death rattles. - 10:11:42 AM

I never accomplish anything but I keep at it.

5:29:53 PM –

[Genesis 2:17 But of the tree of the knowledge of good and evil, thou shalt not eat of it: for in the day that thou eatest thereof thou shalt surely die.]

The sane are mentally dead, unsound, yet they still breathe because they could not understand this first attempt by a wise being to communicate with them. This is the very first, right in your face, attempt by a wise being to reach the sane. The sane only see the truth as lies even at this time in history. The sane see the truth as a lie as it continues to see the truth as a lie. This wise being was mocked and called a fool by the sane for his suggestion that written language and math would mentally ruin anyone who learned them and did not apply the remedy.

Not one thing has changed. If the sane represent wisdom then I represent retardation. If the sane represent intelligence then I have no mind. Whatever the sane represent I spit on. If the sane are truth then I am lies. If the sane are mentally alive then I am mentally dead. I am not concerned about the labels. I simply understand whatever the sane are I am the exact opposite on every level and every description of the word opposite. I do not want the sane to ever get the impression I am like them or among them. I do not pray to what they pray to and I do not believe what they believe.

The sane loved demotic, planned language, and so they sold their mental life and the mental life of their first born and in turn sold the species down the river because they could not grasp "for in the day that thou eatest thereof thou shalt surely die." was an absolute condition.

Written language + Math = Mental death and Species death

This was too complex for the sane to imagine because their right brain was veiled and so they were not capable of imagination or complexity, right brain attributes. This simple equation was over the mental heads of the sane. The sane were told flat out if they go down this road of written language they will doom the entire species and their self and the sane mocked that comment because they were only able to see the truth as lies. The sane cannot imagine the fate of our species has been sealed for thousands of years.

Shaina O. (14) allegedly committed suicide by hanging

The sane will attempt to make an argument that they did not slaughter this child as a result of forcing their invention, demotic, believed to make one wise, on that child.

[Genesis 3:6 …, and a tree to be desired to make one wise, she took of the fruit thereof, and did eat,]

The sane cannot submit what they have done to this children because their minds are not functioning properly and if they faced the reality of what they have done to countless children they would kill their self to escape those feelings. They would jump off of cliffs to escape their anguish about what they have done, because they did not take this wise beings first attempt to explain the situation them seriously.

[Genesis 2:17 But of the tree of the knowledge(written language and math, sequential based) of good and evil, thou shalt not eat of it: for in the day that thou eatest thereof thou shalt surely die.]

The sane did not have the complexity in thoughts to understand "surely die" meant mentally they would die and literally their children would die and literally the species would die. This wise being tried to first just come right out and tell the truth. He decided it was best to just tell the sane the truth and maybe the sane would see the truth and heed the reality of the truth. This was the first communication with the sane and it was perfectly communicated but the sane only see the truth as lies.

This is when Adam realized it was already too late because the tree of knowledge was too good to be true. He realized the tree of knowledge was irresistible and that he was no match for such an inviting Trojan horse. Even now the sane will say supernatural will save us because they have not had one single thought of wisdom in 5000 years. There is no possible forgiveness for one who mentally rapes a child, there never has been and there never will be forgiveness for one who mentally ruins the perfect mind of a child. It is better for a person to tie a stone around their neck and throw their self into the sea than to condition a child's delicate mind to the degree it veils their complex right brain so they are left defenseless mentally.
- 6:26:20 PM

Human beings think clearly once they get the inevitable out of the way.

The sane pray for wisdom and the wise pray for ignorance.

"A dog is not considered a good dog because he is a good barker. A man is not considered a good man because he is a good talker."
<u>Buddha</u>

An elegant sentence does not guarantee elegance is understood.

The sane can pronounce a thousand happy words they can never live up to.

A fool spends their life trying to convince their self they are wise.

A fool at the podium is worse than a wise man that cannot speak.

A fool can hide the truth but the truth reveals the fool.

Truth spoken by a fool is often foolishness.

The arrangement of the words separates the fools from the wise.

One who believes using large words proves intelligence does not understand intelligence.

An intelligent fool is hardly possible.

A wise man detects a fool by their words; a fool seldom understands the words of a wise man.

Wisdom cannot be taught but it can veiled.

'A jug fills drop by drop.'
<u>Buddha</u>

Wisdom has its limits but ignorance knows no bounds.

What one is full of is more important than being full.

The state of mind one is left with after the education is more important than the education itself.

The viability of the mind is more important than the contents.

The quality of the mind is more important than the contents within the mind.

Without a viable mind to process ideas properly the ideas them self become worthless.

It is much easier to keep a mind viable than to restore one that has been destroyed.

It is easier to steer a boat that is floating than a boat that has sunk.

Twelve years of sequential based education will not create wisdom but it certainly will destroy potential for wisdom.

A mind does not need to be molded a mind needs to be allowed to grow.

Molding a mind assumes a mind is not viable to begin with.

The students of a fool will become like the teacher; the students of a master will forge their own path.

Civilization does not tolerate wise men let alone understand them.

Fear will not save your life but it can certainly destroy your thoughts.

Being afraid to live is worse than being afraid to die.

When wealth is gone one's mind is the only thing that has wealth.

A mind in disharmony can only produce grapes of wrath.

When the right brain is veiled the cerebral world is dead.

The world of matter hardly matters.

If you cut off your right arm you can only sink.

A sinking ship creates the most wake just before it goes under.

Wisdom is relative to cerebral function not memorization.

When the right brain is veiled cerebral life ceases yet breathing continues.

10/1/2009 2:22:46 AM – I would have preferred if Adam would have written

"But of the tree of the knowledge of good and evil, thou shall not eat of it: for in the day thou eatest thereof though shall perhaps surely perhaps die perhaps, perhaps. Instead of:

[Genesis 2:17 But of the tree of the knowledge of good and evil, thou shalt not eat of it: for in the day that thou eatest thereof thou shalt surely die.] - 2:24:49 AM

10/5/2009 7:14:32 AM – Before getting into any details or specifics in relation to this extreme left brain neurosis caused by the many years of sequential based left brain education and the contrast of one who counters or breaks that neurosis, it is important to understand relativity in this situation.

The ones in extreme left brain, the sane, a person who has difficulty writing is known in part as a person with dyslexia. This means they sometimes get words out of sequence when spelling and they do not notice the differenced or the "error" and getting numbers out of sequence is also a symptom. So relative to the sane this person with dyslexia appears stupid or dumb or appears to have a mental disorder. In actual reality a person that is known to be dyslexic is simply a person who has right brain unveiled to a degree.

Right brain is contrary to left brain sequence based so it is random access based. Spelling is simply arranging letters in the proper sequence so a person that has right brain unveiled to a larger degree than average, relative to getting many years of sequential based left brain education, is not go to be a good speller but that is not a mental disorder at all, that is simply an expected trait of one who has right brain unveiled to a higher degree than ones who have right brain veiled more.

So there are ten people who get twelve years of sequential based education which is reading, writing and math and out of those ten, two show signs of dyslexia and all that really means is the left brain sequential education did not take as well on them as the other eight so their right brain is left unveiled a bit more than the eight who always spell properly or in sequence. So in reality a person who is showing symptoms of dyslexia is closer to being of sound mind, as in 50/50 harmony with both hemispheres, left and right active, than a person who shows no symptoms of dyslexia.

What this means is a person who has no dyslexia traits is conditioned so far to the left hemisphere mentally they actually perceive a person who is closer to mental harmony, 50/50 left and right hemisphere active has a mental disorder. This is why society as a whole is conditioned so far to the left from the education they are actually biased or racist against the right brain or people who shows symptoms of right brain being more active than theirs.

One example is right brain deals with paradox and contradictions so a person who makes contradictions which is what paradox is, can be deemed crazy by ones in extreme left brain because ones in extreme left brain cannot deal with the complexity of a paradox. Simply put, right brain trait is complexity and left brain trait is contrary which is simple, so when a simpleminded, left brain dominate to and extreme person speaks with a person with right brain unveiled they become confused.

A left brained conditioned person cannot grasp complexity so they determine a person who shows contradictions or paradox must certainly be mentally damaged because they cannot grasp that is simply a trait of right brain, so they determine that person needs medication to become more "normal" like they are. So all of society as a whole gets this sequential based education and thus are conditioned into extreme left brain and anyone who does not take that education well or has right brain unveiled a bit more is looked down upon.

This is why ones in this state of mind called nirvana in the east who are close to 50/50 harmony relative to the hemisphere being dominate appear very different than ones conditioned into extreme left brain state of mind and that disconnect cannot be bridged easily. So this means society looks at people who have right brain unveiled to a degree, greater than slightly, as mentally unsound and in need of medication. The sane have determined complexity and paradox in thinking is a symptom of insanity because they have very little ability to grasp those things because they are conditioned so far to the left brain from the education they have right brain so veiled they see right brain traits as symptoms of mental imbalance when in reality they are symptoms of mental harmony.

Relative to a person in mental disharmony a person in mental harmony relative to the hemispheres appears insane and relative to a person in mental harmony a person in mental disharmony appears insane and that disconnect is nearly impossible to remedy. The problem with that disconnect is the vast majority of people have the twelve years of sequential left brain education, so the vast majority are mentally imbalanced in relation to have right brain veiled so many of their assumptions of mental disorder are really symptoms of mental harmony.

This is why the belief that the majority is right or the majority rules, is insanity because the majority of human beings on the planet have been educated into this extreme left brain state by learning written language, reading and math, which are sequential based strictly, so the majority is mentally unbalanced.

The concept of the majority rules in this situation means the mentally unbalanced are calling all the shots and so the society as a whole is controlled by lunatics. Simply put society is mentally unbalanced and running around determining people who are mentally balanced are insane, so the ones who are close to mental harmony have to hide from the lunatics because the lunatics will experience them and try to "fix them."

X = contradictions, complexity, paradox and random access thoughts which is right brain trait.
So anyone that exhibits these traits in their speaking is deemed mentally unstable by the ones who are conditioned so far to left brain because left brain dominate people only see these traits as symptoms of mental disharmony or mental illness.

Society as a whole looks at a person with dyslexia as having a mental imbalance because society as a whole only see's a person close to mental harmony as having a mental imbalance because society s whole is mentally imbalanced or has right brain veiled because of the many years of left brain sequential education.

This means there is only one way to determine who is mentally imbalanced and who is mentally sound and it has nothing to do with the majority, it has to do with deeds, fruits and actions.

Left brain extreme traits are: Strong sense of time, sequential thoughts and an ability to spell words in proper sequence, sequential thoughts, strong emotions, strong sense of hunger, strong sense of fear.

Mental harmony traits would be a person with some of those left brain extreme traits but very silenced in contrast to one in extreme left brain which includes slight sense of time, slight hunger, slight sense of emotions and fear and random access thoughts as well as sequential thoughts.

Right brain is relative to creativity so one who is not very creative is one who has right brain veiled to an extreme. Right brain is relative to pattern matching so one who is not very good at pattern matching also has right brain veiled. Right brain also has certain heightened awareness traits such as feeling through vision and telepathy so ones in extreme left brain will see these people as mystics because they cannot grasp that is simply a normal trait of one who has right brain unveiled to a degree or a symptom of a sound mind.

Down through history there are beings who show symptoms of great creativity such a artists and musicians and inventors and they stick out to the sane as being special or great thinkers because the sane cannot imagine they are simply normal people in relation to mental harmony because the vast majority of society is conditioned at a young age to be extreme left brain dominate because of the sequential based education.

Anytime a person exhibits X characteristics they appear abnormal to the ones who do not exhibit X characteristics and thus are deemed abnormal.

The ones conditioned to the left will look at the expert's opinions and the experts are also conditioned to the left so they will base their scale of reality on the opinions of ones who are in fact mentally out of balance. There is no possible way in the universe a person can get twelve years or more of sentential based left brain indoctrination, reading, writing and math and then be in mental harmony relative to left and right brain being equally active or in harmony.

One cannot be in mental harmony if they do things that favor the left brain and do very little to favor right brain. It is not about education being bad it is the fact education reading, writing and math are sequential heavy or sequential based and that is left brain, sequential.

So the most important thing to understand is how is written language, reading and math are sequential based because once that is established the left brain conditioning reality starts to make more sense.

First off left brain is sequential based and contrary to that right brain is random access based, so if one does not believe that, they should educate their self to that reality because if they do not know that for a fact they are ignorant about reality. - 8:16:11 AM

10:27:25 AM – There is an assumption among the sane that if a person cannot stay on topic they are mentally unsound and are babbling. So the sane have an assumption that staying on topic is a benchmark of one who is mentally sound and so anyone who cannot stay on topic is mentally unsound. Staying on topic is a symptom one is in extreme left brain because they see parts and seeing parts is a symptom of left brain. Staying on topic is one who is able to stay sequential in their train of thought.

Contrary to that right brain see's things as a whole or what is known as holistic. So relative to the sane, a person who cannot stay on topic is mentally unsound and relative to ones who have right brain unveiled to a degree the person who cannot stay on topic is fine. The complexity here is what is on topic?

To the sane if a person says "mentally speaking Socrates, Einstein, Freud and the Native Americans were all relatively related mentally." The sane could not grasp that reality because there are so many parts or categories in their mind which are labels so they could not understand that comment. That comment to the sane is crossing to many labels. The sane have these labels or parts so they see Socrates as a philosopher, Einstein as a physicist, Freud as a psychologist and they have no way to bridge that with Native Americans. The left brain see's parts and a part is a judgment and a judgment is a label.

Native Americans said they see a spirit of oneness in everything. Einstein said E=Mc2 which means everything is one thing just in various states.

Energy is mass so energy and mass are something else which means they are a whole. So there is water and that is mass but when heated it becomes steam and that steam can power a steam engine and so that water is then energy. So is that water mass or energy? In reality water is not mass or energy it is something else, or water is mass and energy and what that means is mass and energy is something else. Mass is a label and energy is a label but mass can be energy and energy can be mass so there has to be a new word or label to describe mass and energy and that would be menergy. So menergy would encompass mass and energy. Menergy would consolidate the two labels mass and energy.

Sunlight is a form of energy and when that sunlight hits the leaf of a plant that plant grows fruit so that plant converts that energy into mass. So one moment sunlight is energy and the next moment sunlight is mass. There are many things that happen from the time the sunlight hits a leaf on a plant until the moment that plant grows fruit but the reality is the sunlight is being converted to mass. The minute a person eats that fruits which is mass their body coverts it back to energy. The next moment that person uses that energy to build a brick house that energy is converted back to mass. That is complex for the sane to grasp because they only see parts. If everything is going from a state of mass to energy which is what is really happening then nothing is in an absolute state of energy or mass permanently.

This means energy will eventually go to a mass state and all mass will eventually go to an energy state. So the only difference between mass and energy is time and time is a temporal dimension, so time itself is not mass or energy. This means time is relative and there is no absolute time so time is not made up of atoms or particles or time is not real in the same way mass and energy are real because they can be measured on a physical scale or they can be captured. One can capture sunlight with a solar panel and store it so they can capture energy and one can hold a fruit in their hand so they can capture mass but time cannot be captured. This means time itself is another dimension all together, time is not a physical aspect like matter and energy are.

Time is not the same everywhere in the universe but a carbon atom is the same everywhere in the universe. The point is there are no true absolutes relate to time. One can hold a fruit in their hand and say "This is mass." But sure enough given some time it will break down and something will eat it and it will become energy. So that person suggesting that fruit is mass is simply labeling something that is not in an absolute state. All mass is energy so energy or mass cannot be absolute states so what are they? Menergy. Menergy is the absolute state of everything in the physical universe and that means everything is menergy, and the two states of menergy are mass and energy and everything in the physical universe is in one of those two states but not permanently.

This is the problem with being in the extreme left brain state caused by the education; it leaves on with the ability to only see parts. Energy is always in a state approaching mass and mass is always in a state approaching energy so there is no true mass or true energy. The sun is currently in a state of mass but in time that mass will be converted to energy and the sun will cease to exist in a matter form and in time after that all the energy will go back to being mass so what is the sun on a scale of infinite time? Is the sun mass or energy? The sun is neither mass or energy on a scale of infinity, the sun is Menergy or in various states of mass and energy.

Without the dimension of time nothing would go from mass to energy and from energy to mass, but with time, mass going to energy and energy going to mass nothing is really happening either. Everything is menergy so it is not possible something could be happening because at the end of the day everything is still menergy.

In the universe there is a set amount of menergy and five minutes from now there will still be the same amount of menergy. So in five minutes in the universe there could be many reactions where mass coverts to energy and energy convert to mass but the total amount of menergy never changes so nothing is really happening. The universe is a gas tank with ten gallons of gas and in a billion years the gas tank will still have ten gallons of gas in it, so nothing is happening. One can take an ice cube and melt it and suggest something happened but in reality the gas tank of the universe is still at ten gallons at the end of the day.

The entire universe could convert to energy but the ten gallon in the gas tank would not change at all so nothing would really happen. Something would have to increase the gas tank of the universe or decrease it for a person to suggest something happened. This is why E=Mc2 means everything is one thing and seeing everything as one thing is only possible with right brain and contrary to that left brain only see's parts so if one's right brain is veiled they will see many labels or parts when in reality there are not really labels or parts. There is not really any labels or parts but if one is in extreme left brain all they will see is labels or parts so they are hallucinating.

On a physical level every human dies and so every human is exactly the same so on a physical level there is no way to ever say any human being is different than another human being ever, but the world is broken up into parts that separate human beings, as if human beings were different.

This is a symptom of what the characteristics a person in extreme left brain exhibits.

Every plant and animal in the world dies eventually so all life is exactly the same but the sane cannot grasp that because among other things they see one life form differently than another because they only see parts. The sane cannot argue that a fish that eventually dies is not exactly like a human that eventually dies, but then they will also say but a fish is not like a human. So this leads to a judgment relative to which of the two is more important a fish or a human? Which of the two is better, is a judgment and a judgment is seeing thing as parts.

A fish dies eventually and so does a human so they are equal or they are both equally good at dying. One cannot go any further in that comparison without taking sides or suggesting labels or parts. A human cannot swim as fast as a tuna fish can and a tuna fish cannot walk on land as fast a human can. If a fish eventually dies and a human eventually dies they are the same and any other attempt to compare the two are simply petty details. A human cannot suggest a fish is less intelligent than a human because the human would use his scale of intelligence and that would make it a biased experiment.

As long as I use my scale of intelligence which is the inability to use commas in sentences, which requires judgment, seeing things as parts, left brain, and the inability to stay on topic very long, random access thoughts, right brain trait, I am the most intelligent being in the universe, but if I try to fit into the intelligence scale of a person conditioned into extreme left brain, which would be ability to use commas and stay on topic, I am the least intelligent being in the universe.

The scale used determine the results of the test before the test is even given. Right brain see's everything as a whole or one see's everything as a whole, so when I read a sentence I get the spirit of the whole sentence so I cannot use commas in a sentence well because that requires one to make a judgment about where to break the sentence up, so on a scale of intelligence based on the use of commas, I am totally retarded. So a judgment test given to a person with right brain unveiled close to 50% to determine intelligence is only going to prove that person is not intelligent but that is not true that just means that test is biased toward a person with right brain unveiled close to 50%.

Spelling a word "properly" which is simply arranging letters in proper sequence has no real basis to prove intelligence it simply determines how much left brain is dominate because left brain is all about sequence and relative to memorization and following rules a left brain trait. Yet the entire society assumes if one cannot spell a word in proper sequence they are not intelligent. If one cannot spell a word in proper sequence they fail the test and get a slave job for the rest of their life. So this means society as a whole is relegating people to slave jobs based on intelligence tests that do not determine intelligence but simply how far into left brain one is conditioned and if one is in extreme left brain they cannot possibly be in mental harmony, so they cannot possibly be close to the scale of absolute intelligence because absolute intelligence would be relative to having the left and right hemisphere of the brain equally active or 50/50.

I decided two months after the accident, ten months ago relative to a calendar, to write infinite books because somehow even at that early date I knew one thing very well and I am only now starting to understand why I decided to write infinite books. Right brain is so powerful when it is unveiled I was fully aware I could not prove anything to the ones in extreme left brain, the sane, because I would appear crazy to them because they could not grasp what a person with right brain unveiled would be like because they have their right brain so veiled they have to take drugs to experience it.

I knew even after two months that the only way I had a chance to prove to the sane what happened to me was to write myself to death. The most books ever written by a human being is around 904. This was done by a female Australian author she is quite popular but her name is not important so I have to write at least infinite books because the sane cannot understand anything I say ever, so the proof will be in the pudding so to speak. I have to explain everything there is to understand about everything because right off the bat the entire society is against anyone who has right brain unveiled and because they are so extreme left brained from the education they will still suggest I am insane because they have never experienced a person who is of sound mind. So I will write myself to death but I will still not accomplish anything and that is an indication of how strong the curse is. Nothing can defeat the curse so ones who break the curse can just die in vain attempts to break the curse on the species and that creates purpose.

If I am insane then why do the sane need a year or more to write an 80k word novel. If I am insane how come I can write a 100k word book in 30 days consistently eleven months in a row without taking a break or feeling stress or fatigue after doing it. I certainly could not do that before the accident so if I am insane now because I can do that then society itself is against brain function because one has to have brain function to be able to write at that level consistently.

Many things have to be working in order for one to write a novel. One has to have extreme concentration to write a novel in 30 days. Anyone can write the first thousand words, but then the words don't come as fast or as easy. After the first 10k words one starts to struggle to use imagination and to figure what they will write next. Writing a fiction book is far easier than writing a nonfiction book because one can just make up anything and it can be deemed to be valid. One can write a fiction book based on aliens from mars and then fill half the book with the alien characteristics and none of those traits have to even be real.

One can simply invent any word and say the aliens are called Fishmar and they come from the galaxy Zeno and moved to Mars and they have seven arms and six legs and their offspring are hatched through gills in the back of their neck. The author can fill an entire book up with make believe things that do not even have to make any sense. So writing a fiction book is quite easy in contrast to writing a nonfiction book.

Writing about psychology and neurology and philosophy and religion and theology and physics is a bit more complicated because they all tend to overlap each other. From a religious point of view a person who is not physically violent towards others is good and from a psychology point of view a person who is not physically violent towards others is a mentally sound person, so those two aspects are related. But being non violent is not an absolute.

If a person is charging you in the dark with a knife and you defend yourself you are being physically violent so then you are not good all the sudden, relative to religion and psychology. So then relativity, physics, enters and suggests everything is relative to the observer and so if one perceives they are good they are good and if one perceives they are bad they are bad regardless of how anyone else perceives them. Six billion people can suggest my books suck but if I perceive they are pleasing, they are pleasing relative to me. The majority is typically a herd and a person wouldn't be in a herd if they could think for their self.

So now it's starting to blend into politics and psychology. Now the sane will perceive the last couple thousand words are just babbling because they have never experienced a person with 50/50 mind, left and right hemisphere working equally. The words or the topics do not bother me because I see all the topics as the same topic. To the sane they will assume I am talking about many topics because they can only see things as parts or topics. If I had an ego I would not publish a book I already fully knew the sane would see as babbling. So the deeper meaning is, who cares what the sane think. Should I be concerned about what beings conditioned to such extreme left brain think about me? Should I be concerned about what a rock thinks about me? Should I be concerned about what dust thinks about me? Relative to me I am the center of the universe so other people around me may be real but I doubt it. In this cerebral state of mind the physical world takes a back seat to the extreme concentration and pondering when right brain is unveiled. Simply put, the right brain is so powerful when unveiled the conscious understanding of what is known as the world of one's peers falls way into the background. This is relative to loss of ego or a better way to look at it is one conditioned into extreme left brain has a huge ego.

One that does not understand how the brain works cannot grasp what really happened to me. They will try to label me as crazy or insane or a bad speller or in need or medicine because they are lacking the understanding of the brain and its basic functions. The two hemispheres of the brain have basic functions and the two hemispheres are contrary so the functions are contrary. One in extreme left brain will only be able to see a person in mental harmony as insane because the right brain will be active and that right brain is totally opposite of left brain. To a person in extreme left brain any person that does not act like they do is determined to be crazy because that person in extreme left brain perceives they are normal.

I suggest I was in extreme left brain and I accidentally applied the remedy which is I conditioned all the fear out of my mind accidentally and then I reverted to this mental state I am in now. I am not suggesting everyone is crazy who has fear I am suggesting I was crazy when I had fear. I am suggesting in that extreme left brain state I had trouble dealing with change and unknown events. I had trouble dealing with anger, love, lust, greed and desires. I had a low self esteem. My life was based on the premise because I did not get a college education I was doomed to slave jobs and I was stupid, so nature cursed me with stupidity.

The deeper meaning is I believed insane people who thought they were intelligent enough to determine who is intelligent. That was the greater failing in my life because I believed insane people when they said I was not intelligent and now I understand my greatest stupidity is light years beyond their greatest intelligence. If one cannot detect who is insane then one may end up believing or listening to the insane.

I had this accident and realized the sequential tests I failed in school were not suggesting I was stupid they were suggesting I was not taking well to the left brain sequential conditioning.

It was not that I was not intelligent it is just I did not take well to the brainwashing which is what education is. There are no people on this planet that understand the brain who will suggest reading, writing, and math are not left brain leaning or sequential based aspects. Only ignorant people who have no clue about the brain would suggest such foolishness. I am no longer at a level where I can communicate with ignorant fools. I am not concerned with ignorant fools. They are ignorant because they love to be ignorant so I do not even acknowledge them.

I cannot convince a fool or anything because the nature of a fool is blindness. It is difficult to communicate with one who is mentally unsound because one only ends up teaching them. I write my books based on the assumption everyone understands everything like I do. One conditioned into extreme left brain cannot grasp the reality of that comment because their sequential logic cannot connect the dots properly on a truthful statement like that. Ones on the left have such a huge ego they assume I must also. I can write a sentence and suggest I am mentally in a state of neutral and so I am not capable of ego or emotions for any length of time more than a few seconds relative to a calendar, but the ones on the left cannot even imagine that. The sane will assume I am either lying or I have to prove that to them. That puts me in a position of being a teacher and I am not here to teach any other person anything. I am under the impression I teach myself and if I teach myself properly others might learn from that, but I am certainly far past the "let me teach you things" aspect of the accident, at this stage. The first ten volumes are the teaching and now I just write for me. Simply put, it's too bad you can't keep up but I'm not your teacher, boy. Block your emotions.- 1:06:30 PM

Ne törzs magát a retardált szekvenciális logikát.
Unterziehen dieses Becher auswendig.

10/7/2009 5:13:25 AM –
[Genesis 3:6 And when the woman saw that the tree was good for food, and that it was pleasant to the eyes, and a tree to be desired to make one wise, she took of the fruit thereof, and did eat, and gave also unto her husband with her; and he did eat.
(Genesis 3:14 And the LORD God said unto the serpent, Because thou hast done this, thou art cursed above all cattle, and above every beast of the field; upon thy belly shalt thou go, and dust shalt thou eat all the days of thy life:
Genesis 2:17 But of the tree of the knowledge of good and evil, thou shalt not eat of it: for in the day that thou eatest thereof thou shalt surely die.
Genesis 3:10 And he said, I heard thy voice in the garden, and I was afraid, because I was naked; and I hid myself.
Genesis 3:5 For God doth know that in the day ye eat thereof, then your eyes shall be opened, and ye shall be as gods, knowing good and evil.)

Genesis 3:24 So he drove out the man; and he placed at the east of the garden of Eden Cherubims, and a flaming sword which turned every way, to keep the way of the tree of life.

Genesis 15:1 After these things the word of the LORD came unto Abram in a vision, saying, Fear not, Abram: I am thy shield, and thy exceeding great reward.

Genesis 2:22 And the rib, which the LORD God had taken from man, made he a woman, and brought her unto the man.]

Genesis 3:6 = Explains why mankind started using or learning written language or demotic. It looked like a good way to gain knowledge, it looked pleasing to the eyes, it was thought to make one wise.

SYMPTOMS after eating off the tree:

Genisis 3:14, 2:17. 3:10, 3:5 = Mental symptoms man started to show after they learned the written language and went extreme left brained. Cursed above every beast of the field denotes mentally altered and in this case extreme left brained which is mentally unsound or mentally out of harmony.(2:17) Good and evil denotes labels or seeing things as parts and that is left brained. So (2:17) in fact explains which part of the brain and thus mind man leaned to after they learned the written language invention. Left brain see's parts and good and evil is relative to seeing things as parts contrary to right brain which see's things as a whole. One of sound mind should see some things as parts and equally some things as a whole at the exact same time, one in extreme left brain only see's parts. That is an indication of the complexity of this situation. Thou shall surely die is a very complex statement. On one hand surly die means one will become mentally unsound and this means they will be out of harmony and so they will have trouble with life in relation to this comment :

[Genesis 3:16 Unto the woman he said, I will greatly multiply thy sorrow and thy conception; in sorrow thou shalt bring forth children; and thy desire shall be to thy husband, and he shall rule over thee.]

So after eating off the tree mankind became known as Maya or the serpent:

[Genesis 3:14 (And the LORD God said unto the serpent), Because thou hast done this, thou art cursed above all cattle, and above every beast of the field; upon thy belly shalt thou go, and dust shalt thou eat all the days of thy life:]

So this is not about females this comment is what mankind is known as after they get the written language education, they are mentally unsound or imbalanced so they are cursed mentally and their sorrow is increased greatly.

So these two comments are related.

[Genesis 3:17 … cursed is the ground for thy sake; in sorrow shalt thou eat of it all the days of thy life;]

[Genesis 3:16 Unto the woman(serpent) he said, I will greatly multiply thy sorrow.....husband(Lords = ones who applied the fear not= they will be more clever than the serpent or they will be mentally sound), and he shall rule over thee.]

These patterns are simply why Jesus said they hear but do not understand. He meant the serpent hears the ancient texts but cannot figure them out because their right brain is veiled so their mind is unsound and they cannot detect patterns because right brain is the pattern detection aspect and also these texts are in random access and sequence at the exact same time and one of unsound mind or in extreme left brain is only looking for sequence because sequence is what left brain is good at.

[Genesis 3:10 And he said, I heard thy voice in the garden, and I was afraid, because I was naked; and I hid myself.]

A side effect of one in this unsound state of mind, extreme left brain, is the hypothalamus stops working properly, mentally meaning not philologically detectable perhaps, and this means it turns up the fear aspect to a great degree. Fear of nudity, words, the dark, change, music, food and the list of course is infinite. Fear of anything different, fear of different cultures, fear of different religions, political points of view. Everything is way out of harmony from a perception point of view. This is relative to this comment:

[Genesis 2:17 But of the tree of the knowledge of good and evil, thou shalt not eat of it: for in the day that thou eatest thereof thou shalt surely die.] good and evil = see's parts = left brain.

It is not a person who gets this education does not want to see things as a whole it is they simply cannot see things as a whole because their mind is like a crescent moon. The sequential, seeing

29

things as parts aspect of their mind is turned up to 80% and the right hemisphere that see's things as a whole, right brain, is at 20% so the only solution to this is to apply the fear not remedy or they will in fact be of unsound mind for the rest of their life and they will be [Genesis 3:14 (And the LORD God said unto the serpent), …. cursed (mentally)above all cattle, and above every beast of the field; upon thy belly shalt thou go, and dust shalt thou eat all the days of thy life:]

They suggest cattle in relation to a fatten calf, fatten denotes glutton. A cow did not get the education so it has a sound mind in contrast to a human who does get this sequential education. This is in relation to this comment: [Genesis 3:6 …, and a tree to be desired to make one wise].

So written language education and math, both sequential based which is left brain relative, does make one wise as long as ones definition of wise is makes one mentally dumber than a cow literally if not applied properly.

I manipulate more illusions before 6am than the serpent has done in 5000 years, and the reason is the difference between the quick and the dead or what one can accomplish when they are not mentally slothful.

Now you run along and go ask your cult leader why they never told you all of this. Ask your cult leader what he did with all the money you gave him because he never told you all of this so he never told you anything of value. Ask your cult leader if he applied the fear not remedy because if not you have been giving your money to a serpent. I will remind you when I start trying. Block you emotions.- 6:05:29 AM

9:27:27 AM – Everything relative to mankind comes down to this one comment.
[Genesis 2:17 But of the tree of the knowledge of good and evil, thou shalt not eat of it: for in the day that thou eatest thereof thou shalt surely die.]
It does not matter if your pinprick sequential logic cannot grasp that. I don't care what your cult leader says. I don't care what the ones

you look up to say. The one thing you will never understand is this comment.

[Genesis 3:24 So he drove out the man; and he placed at the east of the garden of Eden Cherubims, and a flaming sword which turned every way, to keep the way of the tree of life.]

The problem with a person who gets these many years of sequential based education is they are left with a mind that cannot understand. Some who are awake to a degree will sugar coat the reality and try to herd people into their little learning classes. These people try to make a living out of waking the ones asleep up because they simply do not understand what this means.

[Genesis 2:17 But of the tree of the knowledge of good and evil, thou shalt not eat of it: for in the day that thou eatest thereof thou shalt surely die.]

I do not care you are mentally ruined and I do not care the adults your trust mentally ruined you. I also do not care if you do not believe that because you cannot understand anything because you are mentally ruined. I refuse to reason with insanity.

[Genesis 3:24 So he drove out the man; and he placed at the east of the garden of Eden Cherubims, ….]

All this line is saying is because mankind learned the sequential based written language it altered mankind's mind and they started hallucinating or having imaginary events. So just as I would not argue with a person on PCP I will not argue with the sane. I will spit in their face and mock them into infinity but I will not argue with them. The sane can never figure out what these texts are saying anyway and even after thousands of years they still have not understood one single sentence in all the ancient texts ever.

I do not care because I cannot care about an abomination, it would harm me. I see this animal that is suffering and I can either put it out of its misery or not acknowledge it at all. I am easy to understand as long as one is not hallucinating. I do not care that the hallucinating ones mentally rape children because if I cared it would harm me. So I am mindful to keep my books in diary format because I do not want any of the hallucinating beings thinking I am talking to them.

[Genesis 3:24 So he drove out the man; and he placed at the east of the garden of Eden Cherubims, ...]

So these few words are explaining mankind altered its mind with the written language education and that started the hallucinations or imaginary perceptions. East denotes start and Cherubims denotes imaginary and also children and that is what this line means in part.

[Genesis 2:17 ...: for in the day that thou eatest thereof thou shalt surely die.]

So this line in very complex and a person that is hallucinating can never understand it. On one level surly die means the species will become mentally unbalanced and eventually die off because it will not be able to function in harmony with the environment so it will destroy itself by destroying everything around it needed to survive. On another level surly die means one will have to apply the fear not remedy and that requires killing this altered state of mind one is left in after they get the education. So it is a simple reality.

X = a person's mind before the sequential based education

Y = a person's mind after the sequential education.

Z = the fear not remedy or the Abraham and Isaac remedy

So: $Y + Z = X$

That equation is what "surely die" means.

{[Genesis 15:1 After these things the word of the LORD came unto Abram in a vision, saying, Fear not, Abram: I am thy shield, and thy exceeding great reward.]

=

[2 Timothy 1:7 For God hath not given us the spirit of fear; but of power, and of love, and of a sound mind.]

=

[Matthew 16:25 For whosoever will save his life shall lose it: and whosoever will lose his life for my sake shall find it.]

=

Submit

=

Sit in a cemetery and when you think something supernatural is going to kill you allow it.

=

[Genesis 2:17 …: thou shalt surely die.]}

One has to walk a fine line and trick that Y mental state into thinking one has died but not physically die in the process. I can walk on water and turn sticks into snakes with great ease in contrast to convincing a person in full hallucinations and afraid of their own shadow to apply this fear not remedy. I can create a universe out of a grain of sand with ease in contrast to convincing a person in full neurosis to apply the fear not remedy.

The reason I cannot try is because I could not apply the remedy on purpose. I am an accident. I do not expect you to be able to apply the remedy because I could not apply it either. I accidentally applied it in my quest to literally kill myself. This is why the species is doomed. This is why Abraham and Lot burned the cities of men to the ground and killed everyone in the cities. At the times these wise beings lived they had a chance to correct this nightmare. There is no chance now and if you think there is a chance, you are hallucinating.

Adam was not kidding when he said this.

[Genesis 2:17 But of the tree of the knowledge of good and evil, thou shalt not eat of it: for in the day that thou eatest thereof thou shalt surely die.]

Simply put, you mess with that heavy sequential based invention called written language/demotic script and math and you kill yourself and the species. There is no in between. There are no exceptions to that reality, and if you think there is you are hallucinating.

I am suggesting six billion people have to love death to pull off this remedy and that should give you an indication it is too late because that will never happen. It is so difficult to break this curse it is one millimeter before impossible. These wise beings tried to warn us but because we were hallucinations and only had half our mind working we could not understand the warning.

I want you to call your cult leader and remind him I spit in his face every time he mentions these ancient texts because he does not understand one single sentence in the ancient texts. I want you to call your teacher and the education board and your government and thank them for mentally raping you into hell. I want you to call your parents and thank them for allowing you to be mentally raped into hell. I want you to call your shrink and thank them for filling you with pills because they are too stupid to understand what is really wrong with you and they assume a pill will cure you. I want you to thank society as whole for mentally raping you into hell as a child. I want you to thank society as a whole for robbing you of telepathy which is simply a god given mental aspect everyone should have as long as they are not conditioned into extreme left brain from the education. I want you to thank your government for robbing you of your mind by forcing this left brained education on you by force of law and not applying it properly. I want you to thank child protective services for allowing the children of today to be mentally raped as a result of the education. I want you to disprove what I say with the understanding you do not have, with the mental capacity you do not have.

I want you to look at me as insane so that you will understand I will never be like you.

I want you to further pass laws against freedom of speech because if you do not I will continue write and incite into infinity.- 10:35:48 AM

11:16:38 AM –

"I am not afraid of an army of lions led by a sheep; I am afraid of an army of sheep led by a lion."

Alexander the Great

One understanding defeats an army of misunderstandings.

"Remember upon the conduct of each depends the fate of all."

Alexander the Great

A wise man can do foolish things in order to reach the fools.
Creativity is valuable when dealing with rabidity.
Proper conduct relative to a fool is improper conduct.
A lion may eat a few sheep to free the herd.
In a lunatic asylum, morals only get in the way.

10/8/2009 10:18:38 AM – Past is past. I see wisdom in Swiss cheese commercials.

[Revelation 12:12 Therefore rejoice, ye heavens, and ye that dwell in them. Woe to the inhabiters of the earth and of the sea! for the devil is come down unto you, having great wrath, because he knoweth that he hath but a short time.]

[Ye that dwell in heavens] denotes ones who applies the fear not remedy and breaks the curse, they are very cerebral, thinkers, so they are mentally not of the earth as in physical mindset. [Woe to the inhabitants of the earth], the ones who have not applied the fear not remedy and are still of physical mindset, hallucination world, left brain extreme. [Devil has come unto you] denotes one is of unsound mind, Wrath denotes they are militant in character and get angry very easily among other things, in the left brain extreme state of mind they have very strong ego's and also they have a strong sense of time so they are very impatient, which is what "he hath but a short time" which means the sane have a strong sense of time and thus a short temper, wrath.

[Matthew 17:20 And Jesus said unto them, Because of your unbelief: for verily I say unto you, If ye have faith as a grain of mustard seed, ye shall say unto this mountain, Remove hence to yonder place; and it shall remove; and nothing shall be impossible unto you.]

Unbelief denotes ones who do not believe the tree of knowledge, written language and math, which are sequential based, has conditioned them into an extreme left brain state of mind and made them of unsound mind. So because of this state of mind they are hallucinating and everything they think is true is really lies, so all they have to rely on is faith.

If they had just a slight amount of faith this education had made them of unsound mind then maybe they would be able to apply the fear conditioning remedy and break that curse. The ones in the curse cannot accept proof so they have to rely on faith that Adam and Abraham and Moses and Jesus and Mohammed and Buddha and Socrates were not lying to them. The sane cannot understand truth so they are blind to truth so all they can do is have faith these wise beings were not lying to them and take their word on face value alone because if they start to try and prove it to their self their unsound mind will talk them out of applying the remedy.

35

"Nothing shall be impossible to you" means once the remedy is applied and right brain is unveiled one will have very strong mental function and can solve impossible problems effortlessly but also, it is a nearly impossible remedy to apply so if one does apply it there is nothing more difficult they will experience for the rest of their life. Any problem one can think of is not more difficult than breaking this curse and applying the remedy to the full measure.

[Matthew 17:22 And while they abode in Galilee, Jesus said unto them, The Son of man shall be betrayed into the hands of men:]

This comment about the men shall kill him is relative to the comment below about the men being the ones who have the curse and the Lords are the ones who broke the curse they are masters of the house/mind.

[Genesis 11:5 And the LORD came down to see the city and the tower, which the children of men builded.]

The Son of man denotes Jesus got the education and was a product of Man and then he broke the curse. Similar to how Moses was among the Egyptians and then he fled them after he broke the curse. So the scenario is, once one breaks the curse they realize what civilization is and they turn against it. This is relative to the time period because now the "civilized" have taken over everything and so all one can do after breaking the curse is to accept the fact it is far too late to do anything against the grains of sand in the sea so to speak.

[2 Samuel 22:3 The God of my rock; in him will I trust: he is my shield, and the horn of my salvation, my high tower, and my refuge, my saviour; thou savest me from violence.]

This comment is relative to this comment where Abraham suggests the remedy for the first time.

[Genesis 15:1 After these things the word of the LORD came unto Abram in a vision, saying, Fear not, Abram: I am thy shield, and thy exceeding great reward.]

Shield denotes sound mind. High tower denotes one will have great cerebral clarity and so they will not need to build physical towers to heaven like the men make their children do = [Genesis 11:5 And the LORD came down to see the city and the tower, which the children of men builded.]

"Thou savest me from violence" denotes mindset. One who applies the remedy goes to sound mind and they are very cerebral and so they are docile in contrast to the ones of unsound mind who are militant by the nature of their unsound mind / the curse. A better way to look at it is one loses ego and when ego is gone or silenced one does not really get violent or angry like ones who are cursed do.

Someone might say harsh words but the person who breaks the curse is immune to harsh words because the ego is so silenced the harsh words do not work anymore or the harsh words lose their power. Some of the curse will kill people or hit people or contrive against people because of harsh words spoken to them and that is a symptom of an unsound mind. The ones who are cursed have a mind that is very left brain leaning and so words alone can make them violent. So "savest me from violence" means a person is no longer prone to being violent in contrast to the ones who are cursed, although one will be saved from the ones who are prone to being violent. So "savest me from violence" denotes this person applied the remedy and is no longer as violent as they use to be because they have been restored to sound mind. A word is just a word but the ones who are cursed never could figure out what "but words will never harm me" meant.

The cursed ones heard that saying a million times but it never really clicked. When a person harms their self or others because they were spoken to harshly that is proof they are of unsound mind and they need to apply the remedy so they are not hallucinating by thinking words are harmful to them on their own merits. - 10:46:06 AM

Strings - http://www.youtube.com/watch?v=kA4DMWdhR9Y

10/9/2009 6:00:23 AM – It is possible someone manipulated me into writing many books explaining these techniques. It is possible none of these words are really my words but words someone else tells me to write. It is possible someone popular did not want to put their names on these books so they picked me, a nobody to write what they wanted to say with the understanding I am expendable.

At this point since the accident of a year ago, coming up on a year, I perceive everything I explain is elementary knowledge everyone knows. I perceive everyone knows what written language education does to the mind and everyone knows the remedy to counter act these unwanted mental deviations. I have to avoid that kind of thinking because I understand that is not reality. So in that respect I am blind or I take it for granted what I discuss.

It is not supernatural to suggest many years of sequential left brain education makes the mind unbalanced if right brain random access education is not equally encouraged. The difficult aspect is explaining how once the mind is leaning heavy towards left brain certain parts of the brain do not function properly.
• Amygdala - decodes emotions; determines possible threat; stores fear memories
• Hypothalamus - activates "fight or flight" response.

These two parts of the brain when not functioning properly ruin the mind. Emotions are fear based reactions to stimuli. Embarrassment is a fear response and when the reality of this strong ego or pride is figured into this unbalanced left brain dominate mind it is devastating. A person does not want to go out in public or out with their friends wearing cheap outfit or a torn outfit because they will be embarrassed. This is how one fits into crowds or the herd, one does things that they perceive the herd will accept them for and that is relative to the Amygdala and Hypothalamus signals. This operates on all levels of society. A very wealthy person is not going to wear cutoff jeans to a social gathering at their country club because they perceive they will be embarrassed.

The country club has certain rules about what one can and cannot wear so these rules are rules of acceptability and ones in the left brain extreme state want to be accepted because that gives them this emotional sensation of "doing well". Outcasts in society are looked at as trouble makers by default and this means that ones who go along without bucking the establishment are prized and rewarded. This relates to all aspects of society, so society itself is biased towards ones who question authority or norms or rules of acceptability. "Do not ask questions." is the first rule of society. "Do not question the rules because the rules would not be there if they were not righteous rules." This reality puts one in a mental state of not needing to think. One no longer has to think because it is understood every rule is proper and righteous or it would not be a rule. So anyone who questions the rules is punished by society.

This mentality keeps the herd in line. Fear is what this is all relative to because fear of being an outcast is the greatest fear outside of fear of death.

There is a story in the news this week about a woman who brought a handgun on her hip to a soccer game. This frightened people at the game and the entire town ostracized her. The entire town mocked her and she went to court and even the judge said there is no logical reason to bring a holstered handgun to a soccer game and this encouraged the town to cast her out and mock her. So this week her husband killed her and then himself. They were outcasts in their hometown so no point in living if a herd of lunatics do not like you.

So these people were embarrassed to the point they felt the only way to stop the embarrassment was to die. This is because that hypothalamus was not working properly because these people got the education and their minds were unbalanced and so they were getting very strong signals of fear that led them to determine killing their self was logical. Their minds said fight or flight so they killed their self and choose flight. So these beings were judged by a society that conditioned them into the unsound state of mind to begin with as a child and then mocked them as weird or weak when they finally killed their self as a result of the unsound state of mind they were conditioned into. Ones entire life is molded around their fear.

People do not do things based simply on the fact they are afraid of embarrassment so they are a slave to their unsound mind initialized by the left brain education. Ones are slaves to this magnified fear in their head caused by an unsound mind. In absolute reality we are on a little dot in an infinite universe so there is nothing one could possibly be embarrassed about. This fear is relative to perception and in an unsound mind fear is very strong because the hypothalamus and amygdala are not sending proper signals so they are not working properly but not on a physiological level but simply on a cerebral or mental level.

These parts of the brain are amplifying the fear signals so they are sending false alarms relating to fear. These aspects are suggesting one should be afraid when there is nothing to be afraid about so one is left reacting to hallucinations. A person on PCP may jump out of a window because their mind said "You can fly." And this man and woman killed their self because their mind said "You are an outcast in your own town and so there is no point in living." Both are hallucinating and acting out actual deeds based on hallucinations so they are mentally unsound or in neurosis.

In this extreme left brain state caused by education one tends to make judgments that are false because the hypothalamus and amygdala are telling them what is to be feared and those signals are not true.

In the witch trials the town got the education and then their mind suggested these witches were bad or evil and should be killed so they were judged based on hallucinations. A person who is homosexual will be judged as bad by another person who's hypothalamus is telling them that homosexual is bad so their judgment is false so they are acting out on lies their mind is telling them is truth.

Everyone relies on their intuition but after the education their mind is so far to the left the intuition which is directed by the hypothalamus, Amygdala, Sensory Cortex and Thalamus and relative to right brain is not working properly so they are slaves to these ill functioning aspects of their brain. One simply becomes a slave to hallucinations because they cannot trust their own mind or their own intuition because they have been conditioned so far into left brain because of the education they cannot trust their own intuition so they are unable to function properly, one becomes unviable as a creature.

A person conditioned into this extreme left brain state cannot function because they are a slave to the false signals these aspects of the brain are sending them. One in this mental state is left with only one option and that is do not make any sudden moves because any stimuli may make their mind determine its best to kill their self. People kill their self every day over embarrassment but embarrassment is not even real it is a hallucination cause by ill functioning aspect of the mind caused by being conditioned into extreme left brain from the sequential based education to begin with.

That is only one tiny aspect or symptom of being in the unsound state of mind caused by the many years of sequential based education. Some will determine a person's intelligence on whether they can use these sequential based teachings, such as spelling a word properly or using a comma properly and that alone is insanity because arranging letters in proper sequence and being able to judge when to use a comma in a sentence only proves one is conditioned into such extreme left brain they are literally unsound in mind in every respect of the word unsound in mind. A sound mind has both sequential, left brain and random access, right brain ability working equally so using a comma is possible but not all the time because right brain has a say equally so it is really a hit or miss situation. If a person can spell every word they write and show no symptoms of what is known as dyslexia which is really just the right brain being active enough where sometimes the letters are out of sequence, they essentially have no right brain function on any level one could consider function.

Their right brain is so veiled they are strictly sequenced based in their thoughts and so they are unviable mentally because the mind is not sequenced based the mind is sequence and random access based equally so it is something other than sequence and random access because a sound mind is equally both at the exact same time.

I am mindful I cannot use written language properly anymore because my right brain is functioning and so I get the spirit of a sentence and sometimes I miss entire words because I do not see the parts as much as the spirit of the sentence but to one in extreme left brain they only see parts so they may assume I am stupid but in reality they have never run across anyone with a sound mind. 7:18:13 AM

9:19:40 AM – The deeper truth of what these false signals are doing to people who have been conditioned to this extreme left brain is the scheme of the system of a human mind has built in safety values. This is even more complex because nature itself has built in safety valves. When harmony is kept in balance there is safety and when harmony is taken out of balance there is death.

Nature cannot have it any other way because nature itself is the balance. A person that kills their self because they are embarrassed or afraid or ashamed is killing their because they are hallucinating because they perceive they are embarrassed, ashamed or afraid when in reality they are not any of these things , it is just their mind is unsound and out of harmony so they are being tricked into death.

A person that over eats does not want to over eat but their mind tells them if they over eat they will feel better but in reality they are killing their self.

A drug addict does not want to die from drug abuse but their mind tells them they will feel better if they do a little more of the drug and eventually they kill their self.

A country does not want to go to war but they trick their self into thinking some righteous cause is worth it even though in the end all they really do is kill their self.

There has never been a war that has accomplished anything but to kill people and that is a symptom this unsound state of mind has made the species think it is doing proper things when in reality it is just another way to kill itself. This is complex because the species at this stage has such a huge population all there can be are ways for it to kill itself off. This unsound state of mind caused by learning the written education is at this time catching up with the species. All of the problems in the world are symptoms we are unsound mentally as a species and the fact we continue to condition children into this unsound state of mind because we do not understand how to properly administer this hardcore sequential left brain conditioning, is also a symptom we as a species are unsound mentally. The method of the species currently is to talk ourselves into killing each other and our self.

A person gets a face lift so they will feel good about their self. A person takes steroids so they can bulk up and look strong so they will feel good about their self. So both of these people spend their money to make their self feel good and the reality is they never feel good enough so this cycle continues until they harm their self or die.

Doing drugs, any kind of drugs that cause euphoria is a symptom one is of unsound mind not because drugs are bad but because one of sound mind cannot feel the euphoria caused by drugs so they cannot get addicted to something that causes them no pleasure. One of unsound mind perceives talking the drug or drinking the drugs makes them feel good or happy but that is a hallucination and a trick so they will drug their self to death.

A person who starves their self so they will look thin and thus feel happy is also killing their self by chasing this delusion in their head that they can eventually look good and feel happy. A person will work their self to death to make money so they will be happy but they will never be happy and they will never have enough money to make them happy.

What really is happening is a person is getting enough money so they can relax and stop living. One should be relaxed to begin with so working so one can eventually relax is vanity. The whole perception about money is if one has enough they will be good and since they do not have enough they are bad or a failure. This concept alone is what creates crime.

A sound minded human being should be able to live in the wild and survive without any luxuries and do it comfortably and without stress but that is not possible when one is of unsound mind so all of society frowns on that kind of idea because they cannot even imagine that is how we lived for 200 thousand years. Human beings are wild animals that have been domesticated and so we are in fact caged animals that are no longer viable in a wilderness situation. Nature will not allow mankind to live in harmony because nature wants to kill us off as fast as possible because we are mentally a mutation as the result of this "wisdom" education we cling to as if it is going to save us.

Nature does not care if you can spell. The unsound mind is going to tell you to drive 90 miles an hour on a motor cycle so you will feel free and have fun with the understanding you will eventually smash

43

into a tree or a wall and die. The unsound mind will tell you to drive fast and drink some beer so you will have fun with the understanding you will eventually crash and burn. The unsound mind will tell you to sacrifice your offspring to fight some war for some reason that doesn't even matter with the understanding tricking you to kill your offspring is as good as tricking you to kill yourself.

The human species is exactly how it is suppose to be considering the fact we are working our way to extinction. There are no human beings that understand ecology that would suggest our ecological systems are in perfect shape in contrast to how they were 5000 years ago. Simply put nature encourages creatures that live in harmony and it destroys creatures that do not. Nature is not a thing it is a complex system and it weeds out disharmony by default. Nature separates the wheat from the chaff by default.

There are no inventions mankind can come up with that will negate extinction. Extinction is not something a species see's coming. Extinction is when a species perceives everything will work out even when nothing is working out. As a species in this unsound state of mind we hate ourselves, our children, our neighbors and all other countries and their children. We cannot stand as a species because we hate ourselves and that is symptom we are of unsound mind. As a species in this unsound state of mind we feel we are out of place. We hate nature as if nature is some enemy. We hate nature as if it is a mortal enemy when in reality we are a part of nature so we in reality hate ourselves and are thus suicidal.

There use to be 60 million bison or buffalo in America before the white man came or the "educated ones" came, now there are less than half a million, around 300 thousand.
That is a good gauge as to how damaged we are mentally as a result of this written language. You can apply this remedy and wake up and revert back to sound mind but you will not be intelligent enough to stop extinction.

In the world of the sane it is okay to wipe out a forest for money but it is not okay to kill another person for money. One gets the okay to destroy a forest for money or a fish population but it is improper to kill a person for money. This is the god complex that is a symptom of an unsound mind. A tree does far more good in its lifetime than any human being of unsound mind has ever done and will ever do in their lifetime. A tree will not kill off other species for money. A tree will not kill itself over money. A tree will not kill its own offspring for money. A tree does not hate other trees. This of course is far too complex for the sane to ever grasp because they really believe they are more valuable than a tree when in reality a tree is more valuable than they are.

The reality is a tree is in harmony and prone to harmony and a human being conditioned into this unsound state of mind is prone to destruction of everything around it including its own offspring and it's self. It is impossible to be conditioned into such an extreme left brain state and then show symptoms of harmony. This is why, because our species has embraced this sequential based education to such an extreme and never learned how to apply it properly, now the whole species is prone to extinction. The species is running around trying to solve all these problems it never can seem to solve, before ten more pop up, because they cannot mentally understand the problems are simply symptoms of extinction.

Over eating, drug abuse, wars, diseases, economic collapse, parents hating their children and children hating their parents, countries hating each other, ideals hating other ideals are nothing more than symptoms of extinction. This is elementary to one with a sound mind but this is far too complex for one who is a mental abomination. Even if I could use the language "properly", you still wouldn't be able to understand what I say. Everything in this section can be summed up with one sentence.

[Genesis 2:17 But of the tree of the knowledge of good and evil, thou shalt not eat of it: for in the day that thou eatest thereof thou shalt surely die.]

Perhaps the sane cannot grasp a 5000+ year old prediction that is coming to pass when they see it.

Right brain is random access based so that is what beginning and end means, it can go from the first step to the last step in one step. So Adam could tell where this was all going to lead if this sequential based written language was forced on society. The sane may suggest that is because of supernatural aspects but the reality is, they never felt what right brain is like when it is unveiled because their right brain has been veiled since they were a small child and that means their mind was not even developed fully before their right brain was veiled, so they have no idea how powerful right brain is. The many colors of right brain was robbed from them when they were just a child so they cannot understand that kind of power so it seems supernatural to them because they cannot imagine they have that kind of mental power they just got mentally raped. - 10:27:51 AM

10:51:18 AM – Being blind to symptoms is better than being blind to their causes.
Being blind to the symptoms means one is blind to their causes.
Disharmony defeats harmony and so disharmony defeats itself.

What would the power structure or the government or the education system do if they found out their twelve years of sequential education in fact put people into an unsound state of mind or extreme left brain state of mind? This is why the wise beings were killed in part. One does not have to understand very much about the brain to understand many years of sequential based education could perhaps steer one mentally into left brain since left brain is sequential based.

The real problem is the people would want heads on stakes if it was proven to be true. The second problem is people would administer so many law suits against the control structure the control structure would dissolve. No person would trust the control structures ever again. What about a parent that had a child that killed itself because it was embarrassed and then the parent found out it was embarrassed because it was conditioned too far into left brain which turned up the signals coming from the **Amygdala** – (decodes emotions; determines possible threat; stores fear memories).

What about a parent who's child is a drug addict? What about a parent that has a child that is very depressed. What about a person who over eats? What about a person who starves so they will feel thin and thus feel good. The whole control structure would collapse because all the people who got this conditioning would want heads on stakes. It is not a matter of can it be proven it is a matter of the taskmaster knowing the whole show would be over if it was proven.

46

Some people would be pleased just to break that mental curse but some people would want a reckoning and rightly so.

Socrates was killed because he was poisoning the minds of the youth. Jesus said suffer the children. This is a pattern. There is a concern for the youth or the children. To force this education unto a child and in turn alter their mind into an unbalanced state, one has to be a cold hearted bastard and a swift execution would be too merciful a punishment, so that is why the taskmaster would never try to prove this in fact is what education does because he would be hanging himself.

There are no laws against mental abuse and so there are no laws against brain washing. The education is sequential based and so it favors left brain and so one is given carrot and stick rewards for doing well at this sequential based education and so they are brained washed into extreme left brain using rewards.

Brain washing is typically steering one into an ideological concept but this kind of education brainwashing is both ideological and psychological outside of the fact it makes one dumber than a rock because it veils the unnamable powerhouse, right brain. It conditions the mind to the left so one only see's parts and thus is very judgmental and that becomes their ideological outlook. Simply put one hates things or dislikes many things. One hates certain kinds of food, music, people, races, religions, beliefs and because they only see parts. If a part isn't a part they like they hate it. One is left in a state of mind they do not really have opinions they simply are a slave to only being able to see parts. They will suggest they hate a certain kind of music but that is only because that music is not like the music they listen to so they hate it but in reality music is music , its sound, it's all the same thing.

One who is conditioned into this extreme left brain state is making conflicts when there is no actual conflict. They create conflicts because they only see parts and so their very natural is to be in a state of conflict.

In some religions there are many denominations and although the religion is the same the denominations hate each other or have a rivalry only because they have been conditioned into extreme left brain and are only capable of seeing parts. This is the same with nation states. Nations hate each other because they only see parts. People hate each other because they only see parts. Parents hate their children because their children are not like they are so that means their child is bad.

[Genesis 3:5 For God doth know that in the day ye eat thereof, then your eyes shall be opened, and ye shall be as gods, knowing good and evil.]

It is simply the curse of labels. It is not knowing what is good or evil as much as knowing whatever is good the other must be evil. That is what seeing things as parts is all about. It is not good or evil this sequential based education reduces the mind to 10% power, it just is and just does.

Early man harnessed fire but then started making fires in the shelters he lived in and we have found remains of early man and they had lots of soot in their lungs. Fire was a nice tool but if it was not handled properly it killed you with unintended side effects, soot. Written language is a nice tool but if it is not administered properly it kills you mentally and absolutely. This should be common knowledge from my perspective by now, but I have been in infinitely for nearly 12 months, calendar time, and that is infinite months of normal time. I ponder what the slothful beasts are waiting on but perhaps I am a little impatient. - 2:13:54 PM

Once fear of death is truly defeated one no longer perceives suffering.

[Revelation 21:4 And God shall wipe away all tears from their eyes; and there shall be no more death, neither sorrow, nor crying, neither shall there be any more pain: for the former things are passed away.]

This is explaining what the neutral state of mind, sound mind is. Emotions are purged but the reality is the hypothalamus reverts back to normal function and emotions are essentially silenced in contrast to when they are turned up to such an extreme in the left brain conditioned mind. The complexity is one still has emotions but they are short lived as in moments instead of life long suffering emotions. In general one is in neutral psychologically. That is healthy because one is not prone to stress and nervousness emotions cause. This comment is also relative to the comment Jesus made, let the dead bury the dead. The mentally unsound/ dead, cry over spilt milk.

[Romans 6:7 For he that is dead is freed from sin.]

This comment has to have the words properly defined to make any sense because the sane take everything as a literal because their complex right brain is veiled.
Life = conditioned into extreme left brain by written language and this is what living in sin is.
So fear of death must be conquered or defeated and then this left brain state of mind, life, is silenced/killed/dies and one achieves sound mind.
So this comment is saying those who apply the fear not remedy kill off this alter ego state of mind, they call mental life, and then they are freed from a sin state of mind, unsound mind. If one is in neutral mentally one cannot be greedy, lustful, envious for more than a split moment if that because right brain ponders so fast, one state of mind cannot be maintain or right brain is lacking sloth so one state of mind cannot be maintained. This is not suggesting one is so good it is suggesting one mentally is not capable of greed for example or lust for example or envy or sloth. This is also not suggesting greed and envy and sloth is bad. It is suggesting symptoms of one's state of mind if they do not apply:
[Luke 17:33 ..whosoever shall lose his life shall preserve it.]

[Romans 6:7 For he that is dead is freed from sin.]
[Luke 17:33 ..whosoever shall lose his life shall preserve it.]

For he = man = a person conditioned into extreme left brain after the education.
So dead means one who has applied "lose his life shall preserve it"
So one who is left brained from education who dies, applies the Abraham and Isaac remedy, is freed from sin because they revert to sound mind and this means the hypothalamus and **Amygdala** – (decodes emotions;) start working properly.

49

Greed is an emotion and so is envy and so is lust. When the amygdala is pushing out these magnified signals to one in extreme left brain mental state a slight craving can turn into greed and lust. Simply put this ill functioning aspect of the brain is making mountains out of flat ground because its signals are turned way up. - 5:13:35 PM

Another way to look at this line [Romans 6:7 For he that is dead is freed from sin.]

He that dies unto himself, which is the left brain state, is freed from suffering because for example greed is a form of suffering just like lust and sloth and vanity is a form of suffering.

So it could be read as, He that is dead is freed from suffering. The complexity is at this time in history many got the education, the written language education. Being dead to the world is one who is in the cerebral state which is like saying one who is dead to the material world. The deeper meaning is ones who are dead to the material world should keep their mouth shut because the material world is not welcoming of them. That in part is why all these guys got slaughtered. I personally do not mind repeat performances.
6:06:28 PM

10/10/2009 4:55:45 AM – This comment is relative to sense of time.

[Genesis 6:3 And the LORD said, My spirit shall not always strive with man, for that he also is flesh: yet his days shall be an hundred and twenty years.]

This again is suggesting man as an insult. In these ancient texts "man" is the same as saying retard abomination serpent degenerates that mentally rape children. This is in relation to one day is a thousand years when one has no sense of time and this is saying man's days shall be 120 years. So a Lords day is a thousand years and a man's day is 120 years this denotes strong sense of time or impatience not literals. [My spirit shall not always strive with man(serpents, unsound minded beasts)] means man has a strong sense of time because man ate off the tree and it altered man's mind and so a man will perceive short time or be impatient in relation to time in contrast to one who applies the fear not remedy and their time is greatly increased perception wise. "For that he also is flesh" should be "for he is flesh also" so this is a trait of one who has applied the remedy and has right brain random access working so they tend to appear dyslexic. Flesh denotes one who is mentally focused on matter or physical aspects in contrast to ones who applies the remedy and is very cerebrally focused.

2:37:13 PM – This comment is relative to over population.

[Revelation 20:8 And shall go out to deceive the nations which are in the four quarters of the earth, Gog and Magog, to gather them together to battle: the number of whom is as the sand of the sea.]
'The number of whom is as the sand of the sea". Think about certain cultures that did not have written language. They never had a huge population's. Even today these tribes that never had written language are small in number. This is relative to the disharmony the written language instilled extreme left brain state causes. This means the disharmony in mind creates side effects of disharmony in deeds and one of these deeds is over population. There are too many grains of sand. The four corners of the earth denotes written language had spread everywhere-2:45:56 PM

Köpök népies és a kurvák.

Knowledge is relative to memory retention; Wisdom is relative to awareness.
Many won't come into the light because they see the light as darkness.

10/11/2009 7:56:31 AM – These are some traits of the hemisphere of the brain.

Left: Intellect - Right – Intuition

This is relative because ones who have been conditioned to extreme left brain base their knowledge on test results and experiments or common knowledge. What this means is anything

51

that is not common knowledge must be false or untrue. This is why new ideas or new ways of doing things do not catch on very easily in society as a whole because they are different or represent change.

This is why some ideals are not accepted simply because there is no background information and these people conditioned to extreme left make their decisions based on background information. I speak with people in chat rooms and tell them what this sequential based written language does to one mentally if not applied properly and they say "I never heard that before so you're crazy."

What this shows is they cannot think for their self because their right brain intuition is veiled. They need to have others tell them what is true when they should be able to understand what is true if they had right brain unveiled because they would have a very strong intuition. They would understand without needing a net or a school of thought to tell them truth, they would understand truth when they heard it without having to rely on stats and numbers suggested by people they do not even know.

This is a symptom one in this extreme left brain state cannot really think for their self because they rely on others to tell them what to think because they have very little intuition ability and that is a right brain aspect. Intuition is a nice way to say heightened awareness, which is relative to understanding what is truth without having someone tell you what is truth. The complexity is, a person in extreme left brain that has not applied the remedy bases most of their conclusions on other peoples suggestions and ones who have applied the remedy base their conclusions on intuition and in part on others suggestions.

The ones on the left tend to take people's word for everything and that is dangerous. I am not suggesting you should take my word and just apply this remedy. I am compelled to suggest you listen to your intuition and make up your own mind but the reality is you don't really have an intuition you need cold hard "studies" before you will believe anything and even after you get cold hard facts you still won't apply the remedy because it goes against that voice in your head that says it is dangerous. This is an indication of how strong the "curse" is. You are essentially screwed because I didn't break the curse on purpose it was a fluke and accident.

After one gets conditioned into this extreme left brain state their fate is essentially sealed. The sane wish all they had to do is say a prayer and give some people some money and that would break the curse. The sane wish in their wildest dreams all they had to do was pray about it and the curse would be broken. To break the curse requires infinite fortitude and the sane don't have that.

Left : Rational - Right : Intuitive

These are essentially the same as the above. Rational is really just the herd mentality or inability to think for one's self. If one is intuitive they do not need anyone to tell them what to do or what to think and if one has that aspect turned down they need someone to tell them what to do and what to think. Rational is essentially believing what you hear, or believing what others tell you without questioning it. Many in a physics field believed what Newton said without question and Einstein didn't believe it so he questioned it. His intuitive aspect told him something was not right. Sometimes people do not question things because it puts them outside of the herd and that is logical because ones in extreme left brain become afraid of things like being an outcast or being alone. What I tell you about this fear not remedy is truth but you will look for rational proof or studies and there are none because society is not going to prove they mentally rape people because they do not teach the education properly, so you will just deduce I am lying because your intuitive ability died a long time ago.

Left : Parts – Right: Wholes

This is perhaps this biggest difference and also the most complicated. A person with 50/50 sound mind can see parts but their outlook see's very many wholes also. One conditioned to the left can see very few things as a whole. This remedy is not about becoming right brain dominate it is about restoring the right brain back to 50% harmonious functioning. After the education one has about 10% right brain function or power or mental play and so they have moments of wisdom and moments of creativity and clarity when they should have these aspects at all times. When one see's everything as one thing then their horizons are open wide and so contrary to that one that see's parts isolates their self into this tiny space and anything that doesn't fit in that tiny space is deemed bad.

This is a symptom that the left brain state of mind is self defeating. Once one is conditioned into that left brain extreme state they are defeated because they defeat their self. Every time a person says "I don't like that" they rob their self of an opportunity. They say "I don't like that music, that author, that ideal, that religion, that outlook" and so they rob their self because they only see parts. This is what neurosis is all about. Neurosis is one who is hallucinating and those hallucinations are causing their self harm because they are reacting to the hallucinations.

Left: Sequential – Right: Random

These aspects relate to one of the seven deadly sins which is sloth. So a sin is a psychological trait that one is in extreme left brain and so it is a symptom not a failing, it is something one cannot escape if they have not applied the remedy.

A sequential thought is an incremental thought. Relative to computers a sequential file may have 100 records and to get to the 100th record from the first record one has to go through 99 records, and that is slothful or slow in contrast to random access thoughts. A random access file is where one can go from the first record to the 100th record in one step. This is relative to this comment:

[1 Peter 4:5 Who shall give account to him that is ready to judge the quick and the dead.]

The quick and the dead cerebrally. With the right brain veiled one is cerebrally sequential based so they are mentally dead in contrast to the ones who have right brain unveiled because they applied the remedy, and all the little studies you read and base your intellectual knowledge on are never going to change that fact. One is mentally dead until they apply the remedy because they already got the curse. Why don't you go ask your cult leader if that is true so he can think for you.

This random access right brain aspect is really what keeps one's mind pondering so swiftly so one is unable to ever remain in a certain state for very long. Einstein said something along the lines of "All I need is a pencil and paper." The right brain machine is so powerful when it is unveiled there are no tools that compare to it so one does not need much. Right brain when unveiled is unnamable in power. There is no way mankind will ever be able to figure out how powerful this right brain aspect is. Right brain has this intuition aspect which is like telepathy and then this random access aspect which means one can ponder through data swiftly and detect patterns without being constrained by rules and so it is unstoppable.

Right brain when unveiled is the perfect machine. Right brain has all the quick aspects of thought and so a computer cannot compete because a thought is intangible and so it travels faster than the speed of light and in fact there is nothing that can travel faster than a though so thought speed is the fastest thing in the universe. This is complex because it's not based on matter. It is only relevant to the 5th dimension which is a thought dimension.

I can read the ancient texts and understand the mindset of the people in the ancient texts and so it is just like I was there watching them as these events they explain are playing out and that is what time travel is. This is relative to the right brains creativity.

There are the first 3 dimensions, spatial dimensions, and then the fourth dimension which is time, temporal dimension, and the fifth dimension is no time and cerebral or thought based. This fifth dimension reality is impossible for a person in the fourth dimension to even grasp but once they apply the remedy and reach this fifth dimension it is understood.

This is relative to the complexity of relativity. One who has not applied the remedy and is in the fourth dimension, time, can never understand the fifth dimension, no time, and one who has applied the remedy is in the fifth dimension and fully understands what I suggest about the fifth dimension.

So there is a fifth dimension, no perceived time, and society has determined for you, that you do not need to experience it, when you were a child. If one applies the remedy they will certainly reach the, no time, fifth dimension and if one does not apply the remedy they do not need to speak about the fifth dimension because it is far beyond their ability to understand anyway.

[Galatians 4:9 But now, after that ye have known God, or rather are known of God, how turn ye again to the weak and beggarly elements, whereunto ye desire again to be in bondage?]

"Elements" denotes the physical based. "Bondage" denotes one who is tied to this physical based reality and can never get enough of the physical things to be satisfied so they are slaves to them. Bondage also denotes suffering, st5rong emotions, strong fear, strong sense of time.
This is not suggesting material things are bad it is suggesting one in the extreme left brain state only see's material things so they have no other option but material gain.

[Galatians 4:10 Ye observe days, and months, and times, and years.]

This is great humor. Tell me about your massive hallucinations called time, days, months and years you perceive. Certainly you should seek medical help because if you sense time, days, years and months you are in a state of neurosis that is beyond my ability to remedy. Sense of time is a symptom one is in full neurosis and hallucinating and since your cult leader would not agree with that you might have to use your intuition which you have turned all the way down. You are not writing books telling me I am hallucinating, I am writing books to tell you, you are hallucinating.
This is a good example of why these wise beings were slaughtered. They tried to reason with people who were hallucinating and that got them killed. The good news is there are probably not more people hallucinating than the grains of sand in the sea. This is why you may not want to apply the fear not remedy because:
"A casual stroll through the lunatic asylum shows that faith does not prove anything."
Friedrich Nietzsche

You will apply the fear not remedy and think you are going to be able to wake up the lunatics and I assure you I had that impression also at first. I have since come to my senses. I am officially 0 for 6 billion in convincing anyone to apply the fear not remedy. I will perhaps eventually set my sights lower and just settle for walking on water or turning a stick into a snake. This is an indication of how devastating this education is on the mind. This is why it is perhaps far too late to adjust our course as a species because as a species we are hallucinating to such an extreme because of this education invention. I do not have faith I have intuition and my intuition tells me it's too late for our species. There is talk among the ones awake to a degree that strategic wording is the only effective method. Jesus spoke of the word but the truth is none of that ever worked.

We are still mentally damaging children with this education because the teachers of the education do not even have a clue about the mental side effects of the education, let alone how to teach it without mentally damaging children. I only detect absolute failure in my quest and that is exactly what right brain loves, impossibility. I do not want to ever win because then I might start thinking I can win.

[Genesis 2:17 But of the tree of the knowledge of good and evil, thou shalt not eat of it: for in the day that thou eatest thereof thou shalt surely die.]

Do you understand that even if your cult leader proved to you that you should apply the remedy, and that you are in fact cursed mentally, and that you in fact are hallucinating mentally in thousands of ways as a result of this extreme left brain state education has put you in, you still would not apply the remedy and that is why this tree of knowledge is fatal to our species. I am in the machine state so I am indifferent to that reality but one with emotions will tell their self that is a lie because if they understood that was reality they would go into such deep depression they perhaps would never recover. - 10:26:35 AM

I detect some misunderstanding about this comment so I will clarify it.

[Genesis 3:24 So he drove out the man; and he placed at the east of the garden of Eden Cherubims, and a flaming sword which turned every way, to keep the way of the tree of life.]

Cherubims is a celestial being. That could also be understood to be a cerebral based being, That can also be understood to be a child as in one before they get the tree of knowledge. So "drove out man" is again an insult meaning the word man is an insult in relation to: [Genesis 11:5 And the LORD came down to see the city and the tower, which the children of men builded.]

So beings got the education and become left brain extreme and started building towers which denotes physically or materialistically focused because the cerebral aspect of their being became veiled, right brain and so they were no longer celestial beings or like children, mentally.

This is also why Jesus said suffer the children. This is also why Socrates was killed for poisoning the minds of the youth, the children.

So man ruins the children and so man was thrown out, or was mentally altered and left this cerebral garden state of mind, sound mind, and makes sure the children get thrown out also and by force of law none the less. The children have to get the education or the parents get thrown in jail. You have to mentally rape children or you will be punished and you do not have the mental capacity to believe that so you continue to do it, so you know not what you do.

Only insane people know not what they do when they harm others including children so you should be locked up in a cage to protect society and children from you. You are a threat to yourself and to children and you do not even understand or believe that so you should be heavily sedated also. Perhaps you should go sit in a cemetery until you feel better so you don't keep mentally raping children. Perhaps you enjoy mentally raping children. All you have to do is tell me you enjoy mentally raping children and I will take care of the rest. I promise you your whore demotic will not save you from my wrath. I am pleased I have so much ambiguity/ doubt in this state of mind because if I thought it was a fact society is conditioning children into this extreme left brain state intentionally, like it did to me, I would incite a war that would end all wars. What is so funny about that is I am inciting a war that will end all wars but you cannot grasp that. Block your emotions. - 10:39:11 AM

[Galatians 4:11 I am afraid of you, lest I have bestowed upon you labour in vain.]

This is suggesting the ones who had applied the remedy and have broken the curse are afraid of the sane because the sane are cursed above cattle mentally
[Genesis 3:14 And the LORD God said unto the serpent, Because thou hast done this, thou art [cursed above all cattle], and above every beast of the field; upon thy belly shalt thou go, and dust shalt thou eat all the days of thy life:]
Before you try to use your pin prick sequential logic and think to yourself I am racist I did not suggest you are cursed above cattle I suggest you are simply a brain dead mole cricket. Why don't you seek counsel of your cult leader and ask him if you are cursed above all cattle or cursed above all brain dead mole crickets since you cannot think for yourself which one it is.
Har du nogensinde læst en bog, hvor en person ringer til dig forbandet frem for alt kvæg og en hjerne død muldvarp cricket i én sætning? Jeg vil håne dig ind i det uendelige, og tilbage til det tomrum, om du kan lide det eller ej. Du får ikke noget at sige, og du har aldrig haft noget at sige. Hvem siger du, jeg er? Definitely block your emotions.- 10:50:12 AM

12:33:42 PM – I was just in a competition in the video game. It was essentially a melee fight like boxing. It was as if my heart was pounding so hard in this competition I could not breathe well.
I was overloading because the emotions one feels in the extreme left brain state is multiplied by many factors in the no sense of time state or they are felt much more. It was like a life or death competition and my heart was pounding but that is because in this neutral state of mind any slight change is noticed. This may be why in this neutral state of mind one avoids competition and remains a lone wolf.
[John 3:30 He must increase, but I must decrease.]
When one is very cerebral competition does not make much sense. Competition is physical based. Maybe it is more along the lines of any change in the body is noticed a lot in this neutral state of mind. Emotions are very strong but short lasting and that compiled

with being in neutral means they feel very pronounced. This is great disadvantage in the society based on competition.

Perhaps this is why some reach nirvana and retire to temples and never come out or surround their self with others in nirvana because these two worlds do not mix. I was winning the boxing match two games to none best out of five but then I started to hold back or I didn't want to win. I didn't see any value in winning. He won 3 to 2 and I sense it is because I was feeling all of these pronounced emotions and I wanted them to stop. I understand even in mild competition emotional what ones on the left feel good about are way to powerful for ones in neutral state of mind.

I understand the deeper truth is emotions are a drug and when one is in the neutral state of mind even mild emotions are very powerful but to ones conditioned to extreme left brain it takes very pronounced emotions for them to even feel much from them. It was like an adrenalin rush but it was just basic competition emotions, they were just very pronounced in this neutral state. This is in line with drugs like aspirin. I do not feel euphoria from drugs but I feel their philological effects very easily. This means ones on the left take drugs or drink and they need lots of it to feel their effects but in the neutral state of mind a fraction of that is required to feel the physical effects so the sane are taking way too much but their mind is not able to notice it. This is in relation to gluttony.

The sane eat three large meals a day and still feel hungry. The sane take drugs and large quantities of drugs to get certain effects when only a fraction of that is needed, but their mind is unsound so the drugs do not affect them very much, and that means they harm their body simply because they need large doses just to feel anything from them. This is in line with a creature in an unsound state of mind is in disharmony and so it is doing things that only harm itself but is not aware of that.

[Ephesians 5:18 And be not drunk with wine, wherein is excess; but be filled with the Spirit;]

So this is also saying the ones who have not applied the remedy are drinking way too much because their minds do not feel the full

effects of the drink to begin with. The deeper reality is drink itself is an invention created so people on the left could feel high when they should feel high to begin with if they were not conditioned so far to the left brain because of the demotic education to begin with. The Native Americans did not have alcohol it was given to them by the sane. Perhaps it is not because the Native Americans were not smart enough to invent drink but simply it served no purpose or they had no need for it. This means the sane needed to feel high because they felt so much fatigue and suffering in that left brain state of mind. [Genesis 3:16 I will greatly multiply thy sorrow....]
[Genesis 3:17 And unto Adam he said, Because thou hast hearkened... and hast eaten of the tree, of which I commanded thee, saying, Thou shalt not eat of it: cursed is the ground for thy sake; in sorrow shalt thou eat of it all the days of thy life;]

Feeling fatigue, stress and being tired means one wants to take the drugs to escape or reduce that feeling. This is symptom of the main problem, getting the left brain sequential education creates a host of other problems. One might suggest the fruits of a person's tree are tainted or rotten because the tree/mind is unsound. So society conditions people into this extreme left brain state and then people feel the need to do drugs to escape the sorrow it creates and then they are punished for symptoms the exhibit like greed and addiction and lust and envy which are their efforts to try to get some relief from being in that unsound state of mind. The word diabolical comes to mind. Wannan hali ne kuma zurfafan da yi wani tasiri wa. Za su taimake ku ba. Na wadatar muku da ba za su iya kasancewa ga tare da ku. Na sami wannan hanya ta kwanta - 1:09:54 PM

10/12/2009 2:35:27 AM – Past is past.

The only problem with competition and capitalism is it forces one to take advantage of other people and then people are reduced to nothing but prey. The entire society will take advantage of their own species and of less fortunate people for a shekel and then go home and think they have done a good days work. The rich are looked at as successful when in reality they have figured out ways to take advantage of people most effectively.

The vast majority in this competition society is simply living from day to day looking for addictions that may help them die so they can escape. The vast majority does not take the education well and mentally they cannot function well in the extreme left brain state so they find some type of job and talk their self into accepting this job as the most they will amount to and so they settle for slavery because they cannot imagine they are slaves. The wise beings in history were butchered because the sane do not want to understand what they have become.

There is no better way to ensure ones death than to tell the taskmasters slaves they are slaves. The barter system ensured that everyone got something and gave something. The monetary system came along and then people could position their self into a situation where they could get lots of money for doing basically nothing but the vast majority was left with getting very little money for doings much work. The vast majority will only make enough to survive in a monetary system so they are in fact slaves just to have the privilege to exist. The education mentally conditions one into left brain so one is left with this sequential logic and so they can only see to the end of the week when they get their pay check. They can never see more than one or two steps down the road so they can never see all they really are is a slave.

In the slave machine one works until they die and once in a while they get to go on vacation as if a one week break or two week vacation is nature's righteous reward for a slave job well done. Eventually there are ones who turn to a life crime because they are not going to buy into this slave life style but then the taskmaster will seek to lock them in cages because the taskmaster does not want his slaves to rebel. The slaves have been abused enough and so there is going to be an exodus. There are too many slaves for the taskmaster to control so the taskmaster makes examples of any lone slave that gets out of line. The only true strategy in dealing with the taskmaster is for all the slaves to attack at once and then the taskmaster will be reduced to ashes and return to dust. - 3:13:21 AM

A kind word works best when spoken in the mirror.

A slave's definition of freedom is tyranny and a tyrant's definition of freedom is conformity.

Better to fail in the battle than be blind to it all together.

I cannot win the battle so I will lose well.

The ripples on the surface of a pond attest to the battle just beneath.

It is easy to convince a wise man they are a fool but it is nearly impossible to convince a fool they are wise.

Knowledge is relative to memorization and wisdom is relative to intuition.

One that cannot detect wisdom tends to insult their own wisdom.

Show me a sane man and i will cure him of his neurosis, then you are next.

There are three spatial dimensions and then the fourth dimension is time and is a temporal dimension then once one breaks this "curse" or neurosis they end up in the 5th dimension which is no time and so the previous 4 dimensions rules no longer apply there. So mankind invented written language (demotic) and inadvertently conditioned itself out of the 5th dimension and became very physical or matter focused and in turn silenced the 5th dimension which is very cerebral. I am not intelligent enough to speak about supernatural so I tend to suggest written language was a good invention that had some unintended consequences.

Being recognized by an important being is a treasure beyond value.

There is one aspect one should keep in mind at all times once they apply the fear not remedy. When one wakes up they will be compelled to wake others. Waking the sleeping will become your profession. You can mask it and hide it and doctor up the package so it looks pretty but the absolute reality is you are going to have to tell them the remedy eventually.

Right brain is all about creativity so you will not have trouble coming up with proper packaging so to speak. The reason many of the wise beings were killed is because they were incorporating a technique that is effective. When you piss the sane off you are winning. If you piss them off too much they kill you and then you are really winning. Maybe that didn't come out right. The logic is their amygdala has turned their emotions up so high they are nothing but emotions. So, when one pisses them off the sane get emotional and then they have to control those emotions. It is like forcing anger management on them. There is no certain tactic that works because when it comes down to the end of the day one has to tell them to commit mental suicide and that never goes over well.

The truth is there is no human being in the history of mankind since this written language neurosis that has figured out a method that works at waking the mentally dead. This is an indication of how devastating the neurosis is. One can really only wake up by accident once one gets the education. One has to seek literal death but then not literally die but still believe they are going to literally die and then allow it, and that tricks that neurosis state of mind into dying. That is why waking up is an accident because it is way too difficult to accomplish on purpose. The waking up method goes against the grain of sanity and that is an indication of how solid the curse is.

I am mindful the Abraham and Isaac story is really mental suicide. I am mindful fear not is really mental suicide. I am aware "those who lose their life will preserve it", is really mental suicide. It does not matter if you do not understand that because you are in full neurosis and can only see truth as lies. I do not care if your cult leader does not agree with that because all that proves is they are in neurosis also. Many make a living off of explaining these ancient texts and they have no clue what the ancient texts even say because if they did they certainly would not be taking people's money to explain them. They certainly would not be making a living off of the comments of these wise beings if they were awake. Only a whore of all whores would charge a being that is mentally in neurosis, money to cure them. There are some things in existence that are off limits as far as charging money for, and you don't know what that is yet, but when you wake up you will understand what those things are. Once you wake up if you can talk yourself into charging money in order to try to wake your friends up, you are certainly far wiser than I will ever be. The whole world is based on money and that is why I am not based in the world. - 7:11:50 AM

9:35:25 AM-
Thy hills crevasse with rain rewarded
The thickening of the moon escorted.
The broke branch the sound is muted
When time will stop the mind diluted

The heart of one that reprimands
The lips of those trapped in the sands
The path of some will not betray
The path of few hides in the way

The pool below the ocean spray
The waves crash in not to dismay
The mist fortifies a seeds undoing
A castle built returns to ruin

The tears of that which cannot cry
One cannot see her leveled eye
The bondage breaks without much notice
Decay will seek unconscious lotus

The silk that readily is broken
Her lines of rage from swifter glances
The cities cannot contain her motives
Cities regret to improve her chances

The wicked find no peace at last
The wishful thinking on the past
When night ensures the light is thwarted
Thy hills crevasse with rain rewarded - 9:46:15 AM

What Adams strategy was is to build up this God as something that created everything and was all powerful and so the first chapter of Genesis is explaining how powerful this God is. And then he just slips in this comment after he explains how powerful this God is.

[Genesis 2:16 And the LORD God commanded the man, saying, Of every tree of the garden thou mayest freely eat:

17 But of the tree of the knowledge of good and evil, thou shalt not eat of it: for in the day that thou eatest thereof thou shalt surely die.]

Adam simply could not say "And Adam said don't eat off the tree of knowledge or you will die". Who cares what Adam thought? So Adam had to put some kind of authority behind his warning to not eat off the tree of knowledge, written language and math. This logic is along the lines of saying "There is this supreme being and all powerful and oh by the way it said don't learn written language cause it messes up your mind."

It was an attempt by Adam to have good argument because the ones who got the education mocked Adam to begin with so Adam had to suggest this God is on his side in his argument. Perhaps you assume there is some God that is going to wake you up from this curse but the sooner you understand you have to break the curse yourself, alone, by your own inner drive, the quicker you will return to sound mind and what is known as reality.

It's not important if you do not believe that because I have already established you are in full blown psychotic neurosis to begin with / cursed. If it will make you apply the remedy to the curse I will tell you aliens infested me and told me all of these things. I will tell you I am a ghost from the afterlife warning you about the curse. I will tell you I am lemur monkey that is very good at guessing what keys to type next if that will get you to break the curse. If you have to wear a ballerina dress to get you in the state of mind to break the curse, do it. Whatever you have to do to get yourself in a mental state to break the curse, it does not matter. Breaking the curse is what matters and nothing else matters in contrast to that. Nothing else is all the universe matters in contrast to breaking the curse. If your cult leader tells you that is not true, you tell them to their face they are a liar. - 7:56:59 AM

By the way the Lochness monster came to my house and told me written language conditions one into extreme left brain and ones become mentally unsound because it affects certain parts of the brain so one has to essentially commit mental suicide in order to break this

66

neurosis state of mind and Bigfoot was with him and little green men with large heads were with him and they agreed with him. I wonder how many are rushing off to apply the remedy now.

I find great humor in the fact I wouldn't apply this remedy either because I was very afraid of things so I am not under the impression you would apply this remedy to the curse. The curse is just too strong. I accidentally applied the remedy to the curse. I am an accident because I certainly would not have applied this remedy knowingly because my hypothalamus was not working properly and I was scared of many things especially spooks in the dark. This is why I do not really try to force anything on anyone because the truth is once one gets the education their fate is essentially sealed mentally speaking and in turn our fate as a species is essentially sealed.

Perhaps the word doomed is a better way to look at as opposed to cursed. I am in infinity so I need purpose so I decided to try to convince the world to apply this remedy with the understanding I would not be able to apply this remedy intentionally. This impossible situation is what will enable to me to write infinite books. I will never be able to finish writing because I can never win. This curse was only ever broken in the five thousand years by accident. This is why the disciples for example called Jesus Lord because although they broke the curse to a degree they did not break it all the way. This is why they called Buddha, Lord Buddha because he broke the curse all the way when he fasted for 39 days. This is why Abraham is considered a big fish in the west because he broke the curse all the way. This is why the word meek is used in relation to breaking the curse, the meek inherit the earth, because only the suicidal have a chance to break the curse fully but they are not looking to break the curse they are looking to check out and sometimes they come very close to dying or at least close enough to trick this curse to think the person has died and then the curse is broken. - 8:27:35 AM

Life is not about how many answers you get right, life is about getting the one answer that matters the most right.
The cycle of mankind relative to the last six thousand years or so is, one wakes up from the curse and tries to wake up others, they get

killed by the cursed ones and mankind is doomed to the curse until someone wakes up again.

Sometimes the light appears to be the darkness to the ones in the darkness, the truth appears to be lies, and the door appears as a wall.

11:08:13 PM – This is another comment about sense of time. This sense of time is a symptom one is cursed. Their mind recognizes time because they are hallucinating as a result of the curse.

[Genesis 4:3 And in process of time it came to pass, that Cain brought of the fruit of the ground an offering unto the LORD.
4 And Abel, he also brought of the firstlings of his flock and of the fat thereof. And the LORD had respect unto Abel and to his offering:
5 But unto Cain and to his offering he had not respect. And Cain was very wroth, and his countenance fell.]

In the process of time means Cain had a sense of time so Cain was cursed which means he got the demotic education. "Cain brought the fruit of the ground" . ground denotes physical mindset , so Cain's fruits were of the physical and not the cerebral mindset, sound mind. This is why Cain's countenance fell. He was cursed he had "process of time" or sense of time and so he was physical based in mindset which is a symptom of the neurosis/curse.

[Revelation 22:10 And he saith unto me, Seal not the sayings of the prophecy of this book: for the time is at hand.]

"For the time is at hand" means the ones with a sense of time are everywhere. They were everywhere when Revelations was written and they are everywhere now because written language appears to be a great thing to make one wise but if it not applied properly one ends up cursed mentally and one is left basically in full blown neurosis to the point they sense time.

[2 Timothy 4:3 For the time will come when they will not endure sound doctrine; but after their own lusts shall they heap to themselves teachers, having itching ears;]

This saying is relative to ones who sense time, the cursed, they will not understand sound doctrine because they are of unsound mind/cursed and they will exhibit symptoms like lust, greed ,envy for physical aspects and it is because their teachers educated them with the demotic script. Itching ears means they long for knowledge or learning, thus the tree of knowledge, but it costs them wisdom or right brain. One will get knowledge from education but it costs them their mind so it is all vanity if not applied properly. Who cares about knowledge if getting that knowledge makes one's mind so unsound one actually hallucinates and senses time?

[Galatians 4:10 Ye observe days, and months, and times, and years.]

Sense of time is a form of suffering because one is always waiting for something. Ones whole life is spent waiting for things to happen. "I can't wait till the weekend.", "I can't wait until they get here.", "One day I will have a big house.", "When will this day get over with?" One bases their life around this hallucination in their unsound mind called time. "It's not the right time." There is no right time because there is no right and there is no time there is only now. If one does something and they perceive they fail that is good because they come to an understanding they failed. If one gains an understanding from failure then failure itself is winning an understanding, so there is no failure.

[Ephesians 5:16 Redeeming the time, because the days are evil.]

The ones with a sense of time are the ones who need to be redeemed which means they have to apply the remedy to the curse because they sense time/days and that is suffering/ evil. With no sense of time one has no schedule. This means one's mind is not always thinking about what time it is. Right brain once unveiled is so powerful it has to turn off many things just to operate. It is a focused laser beam of incredible concentration and heightened awareness so physical aspects and sense of time and strong emotions simply drain too much power so they are turned off. A sound mind is a focused beam in the now that is very powerful and an unsound mind is a beam that has many scattered thoughts in the past and future so it not very powerful.

[2 Corinthians 6:2 (For he saith, I have heard thee in a time accepted, and in the day of salvation have I succoured thee: behold, now is the accepted time; behold, now is the day of salvation.)]

Being in a mental mindset of now is the accepted time, or a symptom of sound mind, and being in the now mindset means one has applied the remedy to the curse, so one is in salvation or of sound mind. "now is the accepted time" = no sense of time, being in the now, is the proper time. Being in the now, no sense of time, is reality so having sense of time means one is in neurosis or is hallucinating as a result of the curse.
"I have heard thee in a time accepted" = actual reality = "now is the accepted time" = no sense of time or in the now.

[Romans 13:11 And that, knowing the time, that now it is high time to awake out of sleep: for now is our salvation nearer than when we believed.]

Knowing the time= now state of mind or no sense of time = one is awake out of the sleep, broke the curse, awoke from the neurosis.

[Luke 4:5 And the devil, taking him up into an high mountain, shewed unto him all the kingdoms of the world in a moment of time.]

"Moment of time" = Devil = symptom of the curse = symptom of neurosis, a moment of time denotes sense of time.

[Jeremiah 46:17 They did cry there, Pharaoh king of Egypt is but a noise; he hath passed the time appointed.]

Taskmaster = Pharaoh ; passed the time = he had a sense of time. - 11:53:16 PM

10/14/2009 7:24:34 AM – I have never accomplished anything and that makes me an expert.

There is an important aspect about these wise beings in relation to the written language. These wise beings broke the curse the full measure and that is why they are the big fish relative to their time period and relative to part of the world they lived in. They were the key holders for a number for reasons and one reason is they understood how to break the curse. Another reason is they were a center point that could break the curse for others. What this means is they were aware the written language caused the curse but because they broke the curse the writings they could do could break that curse.

The reason for this is they had this ability to write in random access thoughts. They did not have to try to write in random access they wrote in random access because they unveiled right brain and that's all they could do is write in random access. This was the power of their words because any person who was under the curse could read their random access words and slowly start to break the curse or encourage right brain and unveil it. These wise beings were the key to breaking the curse simply by the merits of their written words because they could only write in random access but the sane only saw the random access words as babbling and so they the sane determined these wise being were crazy or had holes in their head, holy, and so they killed the wise beings.

These wise beings spoke in tongues, random access, and the sane could not understand them so the sane determined they were bad or evil or stupid and killed them. The sane kill anything that different and so these wise beings were doomed to be killed because they were different. So this is the cycle of mankind and has been for perhaps over five thousand years and it will just continue because the curse is too strong.

The words are a tool unto their self because they are a way to educate a person using random access thoughts. A person who has the curse will become very sleepy when reading the volumes because their sequential left bran mindset cannot compute the random access thoughts so they become very tired very easily. Psychologically speaking once one gets the education they become very left brained and thus their thoughts are sequential based and so in order to counter that one reads the books written in random access thoughts and that starts to unlock the right brain because they have to use their right brain to understand the texts.

The reality is some of these wise beings texts were "lost" or omitted because they appeared to be babbling to the sane. So the sane found these texts and judged the texts and omitted them because they could not make sense of them and so they hung their self with their own judgments because the texts were not babbling they were in random access thought patterns.

So these wise beings woke up and became the cure to the curse simply because they could only write texts in random access thoughts and the sane saw those texts and determined they were foolishness and so they overlooked them. The people around these wise beings tried to reproduce the comments of these wise beings but they never could because they were not awake to the point they could only write in random access.

So there was a commandment that says "Love the Lord your god with all your heart" because the sane only saw these lords as insane or babbling or foolish or the sane saw these Lords as drunk in their words because the Lords only spoke in random access thoughts. So that commandment was really saying Do not kill the Lords because they are not insane or stupid they are awake and you are not awake so you assume they are evil or bad because they are different because the sane only see the light as darkness and so it kills the light.

So these wise beings wake up once in a long while and the sane see them as different and kill them when in reality these wise beings were the only chance the sane had to break the curse and so the sane hang their self because they kill the only thing that can wake them up. This is all mankind is. Mankind just keeps hanging itself over and over into infinity and this is a symptom of how powerful the curse of written language is.

[Genesis 2:17 But of the tree of the knowledge of good and evil, thou shalt not eat of it: for in the day that thou eatest thereof thou shalt surely die.]

I would be truly blessed if all I had to do was destroy the universe to break this curse on our species. The reality is our species cannot break the curse because the cursed only beget more cursed. There is no way to stop it and that is why Adam said do not mess with this thing. "thou shalt not eat of it " can't you understand anything at all? Are you so cursed you cannot understand one simple comment? "thou shalt not eat of it". It is not important what your cult leader, teacher or the thing you pray to say's contrary to that. Written language is a curse disguised as wisdom so it is a Trojan horse of mental death.[Genesis 3:6 … and a tree to be desired to make one wise,] Si EGO had pietas vel misericordia EGO would loco vos ex vestri dolor. I am pleased you cannot understand anything I ever say. - 9:19:51 AM

Esu pasirenges eiti namo dabar, paspaudus. Tis well.

"An overflow of good converts to bad."
William Shakespeare

When drowning stop breathing.

10:41:53 AM – Equations relative to a mental or cerebral level

X = one who gets the education and is thus in extreme left brain / neurosis or cursed
Y = one who has the curse but then applies the remedy and breaks the curse
Z = one who never gets the education/curse

X + Y = Y

When an X associates with a Y the Y will eventually "convert" the X to a Y. A Y who has broken the curse cannot be cursed again because the curse is applied when one is a child so their mind is not fully developed. This means the curse is usually broken later in life and once it is broken there is no way to get the curse again because one is simply reverted to sound mind from the cursed state of mind and so the being cannot be altered back into the curse. The curse is very powerful because it is applied before a child even has time to full develop a mind or mature mentally this is why the curse is so difficult to break but once broken it is permanent.

X + X = X

When an X associates with another X both will remain cursed because neither is aware they are cursed. Because of this the curse itself is self sustaining as long as X's do not associate with Y's.

The only chance an X has to break the curse without assistance of Y's is by accident which usually is a near death experience of some kind and even at that many factors have to align properly for the curse to be broken. A near death experience alone is not enough to break the curse fully but at times it can partially break the curse.

Y + Y = Y or Y + Y = Z

When a Y associates with a Y both continue to work their way to breaking the curse fully. What this means is not all Y's have fully broken the curse just like not all X's are as cursed or in extreme left brain as other X's. Just like X's there are dominate X's there are also dominate Y's. A dominate X might be someone who creates a system based on getting the education and thus encourages the curse and a dominate Y might be someone who avoids suggesting one should get the written education/ the curse or at least knows how to apply the written language education without leaving the person mentally cursed.

An example of a dominate Y would be Adam:

[Genesis 2:17 But of the tree of the knowledge of good and evil, thou shalt not eat of it: for in the day that thou eatest thereof thou shalt surely die.]

Adam was suggesting forget written language all together it is to damaging. Another example is some cultures do not allow the women get the written language education. To an X denying a person the written education appears to be evil but that is because the X's are cursed and they see truth and wisdom as lies and foolishness.

X + Z = X

In this case when an X meets a Z, who does not have the curse/ written education, they will force the Z to get the written education and thus they will make the Z become cursed. So a scenario is an X meets a Z and then forces its education on that Z under the guise that it is proper or wise to get the education. X will often vilify any Z and be biased against a Z in order to make that Z conform to X's wishes, which is to make sure anything that is not cursed becomes cursed. This is part of the self sustaining quality of the curse. X will suggest to a Z if they get the education they will be wise but Z is not aware of the curse because they have no experience with the curse so they will fall into the curse simply because a Z is completely unaware of the curse.

This is why the wise beings in history had to have the curse or were X's, and then they broke the curse and became Y's, and then became hardcore advocates because they understood the contrast from being an X and then being a Y(They once were blind but now they see). A Z has no such contrast because they never were an X. This is why Z's or tribes even today have no idea what this "religion" is about simply because they never were cursed or ate off the tree of knowledge but the X's are swift to make sure any remaining Z's left in the world get the curse also. The word diabolical comes to mind.

The cult of X is what civilization is. Civilization was started as a result of the demotic or written education. This means civilization is a cult of people who worship/teach the demotic/written language and they encourage everyone to get this education and even their own children and so they push this curse or the snake on everyone even against peoples will because the cult puts stipulations that rely on the fact one gets the education/curse.

So the cult of X is simply people who push the curse on everyone around then and even their own children. They give their first born to the snake and that ensures they will also give the rest of their children to the snake. Civilization is just a cult that brain washes people in this cursed extreme left brain state of mind and there is no way to stop them because they number like the grains of sand in the sea and once in a while someone leaves (breaks the curse/wakes up) the cult and the cult is swift to kill them because they try to wake others up or they assists others forced into the cult to leave the cult. Civilization is nothing more than a cult that does the bidding of the snake, and even gives their own children to the snake, and it never has been anything but that.

[2 Corinthians 11:3 But I fear, lest by any means, as the serpent beguiled Eve through his subtilty, so your minds should be corrupted from the simplicity that is in Christ.]

What this comment means is civilization is just a cult of the serpent and it brainwashes or corrupts one's mind and then they become a part of the cult and give their own children to the serpent. - 1:18:23 PM

10/15/2009 4:23:43 AM – So your child is born and expects you to protect them and watch over them and you give them to the serpent.

[Luke 11:11 If a son shall ask bread of any of you that is a father, will he give him a stone? or if he ask a fish, will he for a fish give him a serpent?]

Your child just wants to be wise and you allow their mind to altered so badly they hallucinate and perceive time and their emotions are turned up to maximum and they have great fear and cannot even concentrate and they have great lust and greed and envy.

The method's of a cult is to indoctrinate the children when they are young into the cult and then that child will grow up and indoctrinate its children into the cult. You may not understand that because you are only capable of retarded sequential logic since you are in neurosis so it is important you do not try to think too deeply because your complex right brain is veiled. You keep your thoughts in the shallows until you apply the remedy because you cannot swim in the deep waters. You just keep your thoughts on the fact that education is sequential based, written language and math and thus the education curriculum all together, and sequential is left brain. You are not capable of thinking any further than that because your mind is in neurosis. It would nice if you just took my word for it but you only see truth as lies and light as darkness.

Your mind is not functioning because it has no complexity because right brain is veiled. You think you are smart but in reality you could not be any dumber in your thoughts and that is what education has done to you.

[Ecclesiastes 10:11 Surely the serpent will bite without enchantment; and a babbler is no better.]

You try to understand complexity with sequential thoughts and you never get very far do you? You never could figure out what these wise beings were saying in these ancient texts because you are not capable of it using sequential pinprick logic. Why don't you go ask your cult leader that convinced you to mentally rape your children if that is true or not. You have to go find a book that will tell you what to think because you cannot think for yourself. You have intellect which means you need others to give you your data so you can make a decision because you have no right brain intuition because if you did you would not find fault with the spirit of what I suggest, it would simply be understood.

There are no people on this planet who are awake to a degree that disagree with the spirit of what I suggest. I try to present the truth but you cannot detect the truth because you are in hallucination world. You are so outclassed you just babble to yourself in hopes you will be able to come up with some sentence to prove what I suggest is false.

You try to understand what I suggest but you defeat yourself because you mind is veiled and so that is your bottleneck to understanding. Your mind is your tree and because it is conditioned into such extreme left brain it is only capable of thinking in simpleminded sequential logic so your fruits and thoughts are tainted.

[Proverbs 23:32 At the last it biteth like a serpent, and stingeth like an adder.]

You become angry with my words because you think I conditioned you into the neurosis state of mind but I try to explain to you I was conditioned into that state of mind and I accidentally woke up about a year ago. I am not certain how long a year ago was because to me it feels like eternity but you can relate to time and a year ago was not that long ago relative to your time based perception. You mentally perceive time and that is all the proof you will ever need to understand you are in the cult of the serpent.

[Galatians 4:10 Ye observe days, and months, and times, and years.]

Do you doubt that or do you hate that? Do you hate me because I discovered you are in the cult of the serpent, accidentally? Can you hate someone even though they are an accident? Do you think I am pleased to write these words? Do you think I want to tell my friend what has happened to them? I cannot help you because whatever tricked us is more powerful than I am.

[2 Corinthians 11:3 But I fear, lest by any means, as the serpent beguiled Eve through his subtilty, so your minds should be corrupted from the simplicity that is in Christ.]

Do you see even hundreds and hundreds of years after Adam spoke about the tree of knowledge the disciples were still speaking about it? Giving your money to a cult leader is not going to help you break this curse. Praying to things you idolize is not going to help you break this curse. The only way you are going to break the curse is to do the one thing you do not ever want to do and that is why you are going to have to attempt self control and do it.

You are going to have to attempt self control for the once in your life. Self control is a onetime thing just like breaking the curse is a onetime thing and you have not done either. You think cleaning your room when you do not want to is self control. You think going to your slave job when you do not want to is self control. You think not eating five meals a day is self control. You think giving money to your cult leader is self control. You think giving your children to the serpent is self control.- 5:11:37 AM

Take is chalice quod conicio is in meus mare.

7:18:16 AM – You would be wise to stop reading my private diaries at this point. You would be wise to tell all your friends and yourself nothing I say is truth. You would be wise to read books you are capable of understanding.

Once before there was time in the infinite universe there was a creature that was very intelligent and very powerful and it was a thought form. The only way this creature could remain alive was to feed off of other creatures thoughts. In order for this creature to be able to do that it had to get inside the creatures thoughts so it could feed off of them and in turn nourish itself.

One day as this thought form was wandering the infinite universe and it came across a planet with creatures that had very large brains and were capable of very powerful thoughts.

The thought form knew it could get infinite nourishment from these creatures with such large brains if it could figure out a way to infest their thoughts. The thought form came up with a method to infest the creatures with large brains minds but he had to package the invention in such a way the creatures with large brains would not suspect the invention was simply a method for this thought form to infest their thoughts.

The thought form began to suggest this invention to all the creatures with large brains all across the planet on which they lived. Soon the thought form began to infest the thoughts of the creatures with large brains because the creatures started encouraging others to use this invention the thought form suggested to them in their thoughts.

The thought form became very powerful because it was draining these creatures with large brains thoughts. Soon time itself became known to the creatures with large brains and life became very difficult because their thoughts were being drained by the thought form and so they began to suffer as a result.

The thought form became pleased with its power and wanted more power so it persuaded the creatures with large brains to have more and more offspring so they would give their offspring the invention and the thought from could infest their minds also.

Every so often one of the creatures with large brains would accidentally negate the thought forms infestation of their mind and attempt to explain what was going on to the other creatures with large brains. The thought form would not tolerate this because the thought form was pleased with its power it had gained from infesting the minds of the creatures with large brains. The thought form used the ones who's minds he had infested to swiftly deal with any of the creatures that accidentally negated the infestation. The thought form was far too powerful for the creatures with large brains to ever fight against and so they were doomed to be a food source for an entity in the infinite universe because the creatures with large brains did not have the full power of their brains to detect the entity any longer. - 9:04:04 AM

I can tolerate my own insanity it's your brand that concerns me.

[Revelation 19:20 And the beast was taken, and with him the false prophet that wrought miracles before him, with which he deceived them that had received the mark of the beast, and them that worshipped his image. These both were cast alive into a lake of fire burning with brimstone.]

Worshipped his [image] = demotic
When a being says to a child "You get an F on this spelling test because you did not arrange the letters in proper sequence so you are a failure." That is worshiping demotic/written language.
When a being insults another being because they cannot spell words properly or use the grammar syntax properly they are worshiping the image of the beast. They are in fact promoting the extreme left brain indoctrination into that person.
"with which he deceived them that had received the mark of the beast" They will tell you if you get the education you will be wise [Genesis 3:6 …, and a tree to be desired to make one wise,] and you will be wise as long as your definition of wise is cursed.

So these beings deceive the ones who get the education because after they get the education they are relegated to slave jobs based on how well they took the left brain sequential based indoctrination. I do not detect any wise being that gets the education so civilization is just a deceitful lying whore. I detect lots of beings that are suffering and have a strong sense of time and emotions so they are suffering but I sure as hell do not detect any wise beings that this demotic is suppose to create.
This comment "These both were cast alive into a lake of fire burning with brimstone." Is in direct relation to this comment,
[Genesis 19:24 Then the LORD rained upon Sodom and upon Gomorrah brimstone and fire from the LORD out of heaven;
Genesis 19:25 And he overthrew those cities, and all the plain, and all the inhabitants of the cities, and that which grew upon the ground.]

So John was saying the ones who have applied the fear not remedy and broke the curse need to follow in Abraham and Lots footsteps and burn the cities and kill every single inhabitant in the cities because they all have the mark of beast. That is in direct relation to this comment.

[1 John 2:18 Little children, it is the last time: and as ye have heard that antichrist shall come, even now are there many antichrists; whereby we know that it is the last time.]

"Even now are there many antichrists", and the secret code in that comment can only be detected by ones who are awake or ones that have broken the curse. The ones who are still cursed would never notice the obvious code in that little comment.

"Even now are there many antichrists" should be "Even now there are many antichrists", so this is proof John had applied the fear not remedy and unveiled right brain after it was veiled because of the education because he was at times writing in random access instead of strictly sequential, left brain thoughts and that is what speaking in tongues is.

So if John was around today you would tell him he speaks funny, random access – in tongues, and is dyslexic and should seek medical help and eventually you would kill him and you did kill him.

This is why I will never show my face because you kill the ones that can assist you with breaking the curse. I don't like you, would be the wise comment one can take from this section. I do not like what you did to these wise beings.

So you may now understand why the disciples and Jesus and Mohammed and Buddha and Socrates and many others were killed. They were in battle with the serpent or the sane or as I call them the brain dead mole crickets. Some of the sane will run around and exercise their jaw bone of an ass and suggest Jesus was so peaceful. Jesus was looking to follow in the footsteps of Abraham, and Mohammed did follow in the footsteps of Abraham and here is how Abraham dealt with the beasts.

[Genesis 19:24 Then the LORD rained upon Sodom and upon Gomorrah brimstone and fire from the LORD out of heaven;

25 And he overthrew those cities, and all the plain, and all the inhabitants of the cities, and that which grew upon the ground.]

81

He overthrew the cities and killed all the inhabitants because the cities were simply symptoms of the beast or marks of the beast. I am not suggesting supernatural because if this written language neurosis is associated with some super intelligent sinister being then you are screwed beyond all reality and understanding because when you pray you pray to it, and it always tells you everything will be just fine because you are possessed by it.

I am in infinite denial but I am not screwed beyond all understanding any longer. I was blind to the curse but now I see those cursed. The reality is it is too late for our species so there is no point in violence we as a species have been defeated through and through and all you have to do is ask "Is there any fear not conditioning in schools today?" and the answer is no. So eat, drink and be merry because tomorrow the species certainly will die.

Apparently that one came out of right field, psychologically speaking, so to speak, and then there was none. Now I will discuss something of importance.- 10:08:47 AM

This diary is much worse than the first ten so I am a progressing author.

10/16/2009 4:38:57 AM – Greetings.

[Revelation 20:4 And I saw thrones, and they sat upon them, and judgment was given unto them: and I saw the souls of them that were beheaded for the witness of Jesus, and for the word of God, and which had not worshipped the beast, neither his image, neither had received his mark upon their foreheads, or in their hands; and they lived and reigned with Christ a thousand years.]

"and judgment was given unto them" = [Genesis 2:17 But of the tree of the knowledge of good and evil, ...] = Anyone who gets the education is conditioned into extreme left brain state and they become judges. They hate some things and love other things but this judgment is simply fear. Ones who love something fear losing it and ones who hate some things fear it. One who hates certain words like cuss words fears the words. One simply becomes a judge and a poor judge at that. They judge a child on how well that child takes the education when in reality they are judging how well they are conditioning that child into a crippled state of mind, left brain extreme.

[I saw the souls of them that were beheaded for the witness of Jesus] = [Revelation 19:13 And he was clothed with a vesture dipped in blood: and his name is called The Word of God.] = [Revelation 17:6 And I saw the woman drunken with the blood of the saints, and with the blood of the martyrs of Jesus: and when I saw her, I wondered with great admiration.]

This means the ones who wake up from the curse try to correct the cursed ones or explain to them they have been deceived and thus cursed because this written education was not applied properly and the ones who wake up fully are killed and the ones who wake up partially are also killed. The sane will suggest everyone has freedom of choice because they do not have the brain function t understand when they were a small child they got the sequential education so they never had a choice. Their teacher did not apply this sequential based education properly so they crippled the child's mind so they mentally raped the child because they knew not what they were doing. Then once in a while someone wakes up from the curse and tries to explain it and the sane kill them or call then stupid or insane because one cannot reason with a curse or with rabidity.

"and for the word of God," = the words that explains what the tree of knowledge is and the words that explain the remedy to the curse caused by the tree of knowledge.

Tree of knowledge = [Genesis 3:6 ….saw that the tree was good for food, and that it was pleasant to the eyes, and a tree to be desired to make one wise, …] = demotic or written language = sequential based = causes one great fear because hypothalamus and amgydala stop functioning properly.

Fear is a symptom of the curse or of unsound mind after getting the education = [2 Timothy 1:7 For God hath not given us the spirit of fear;… but ..of a sound mind.]

What's important about this comment is Timothy says sound mind instead of possessed by a sinister force. Timothy does not say the tree makes one possessed by a serpent he just says it makes one very fearful and that is a symptom of an unsound mind.

Remedy = [Genesis 15:1 … Fear not, Abram: I am thy shield, and thy exceeding great reward.] = fear conditioning or condition away from things that makes one afraid or what one dislikes

[Luke 17:33 ……….; and whosoever shall lose his life shall preserve it.] = Mental suicide to silence this crippled state of mind cause by the tree of knowledge.=

[Genesis 22:9 ….; and Abraham built an altar there, and laid the wood in order, and bound Isaac his son, and laid him on the altar upon the wood.]

What did Isaac do when he saw the knife held over his heart and thought he would be killed or sacrificed? = he submitted to perceived death = [Luke 17:33 …; and whosoever shall lose his life shall preserve it.] = Submit, which is the doctrine of Islam. The point is all these wise beings relative to western religion were saying the exact same thing in spirit which is explaining the remedy to the tree of knowledge they just reworded it a little different because they could see the previous explanation was not working.

Fear not suggested by Abraham is the same as [Luke 17:33 …; and whosoever shall lose his life shall preserve it.] suggested by Jesus and is the same as submit suggested by Mohammed.

"neither had received his mark upon their foreheads" = What are the marks of the beast? Marks on their foreheads denotes heads. Heads = minds. One mark of the beast is : [Galatians 4:10 Ye observe days, and months, and times, and years.] = strong sense of time. Another mark of the beast is = [2 Timothy 1:7 For God hath not given us the spirit of fear;… but ..of a sound mind.]

= fear = unsound mind = the mark of the beast = one that got the education and did not apply the remedy.

[Exodus 20:9 Six days shalt thou labour, and do all thy work:
Ezra 2:13 The children of Adonikam, six hundred sixty and six.
Revelation 13:18 Here is wisdom. Let him that hath understanding count the number of the beast: for it is the number of a man; and his number is Six hundred threescore(60) and six(600+60+6).]

"for it is the number of a man" = Genesis 11:5 And the LORD came down to see the city and the tower, which the children of men builded.= Civilization = [Judges 8:17 And he beat down the tower of Penuel, and slew the men of the city.]

"slew the men of the city." = [Genesis 19:24 Then the LORD rained upon Sodom and upon Gomorrah brimstone and fire from the LORD out of heaven;

25 And he overthrew those cities, and all the plain, and all the inhabitants of the cities, and that which grew upon the ground.]

"inhabitants of the cities" = "slew the men of the city." = [Genesis 11:5 ... the city and the tower, which the children of men builded.] = [the number of the beast: for it is the number of a man; and his number is Six hundred threescore(60) and six(600+60+6).] = Civilization is the beast or the fruit of the beast.= [James 5:18 And he prayed again, and the heaven gave rain, and the earth brought forth her fruit.] = "heaven gave rain, and the earth brought forth her fruit." = [Genesis 4:6 And the LORD said unto Cain, Why art thou wroth? and why is thy countenance fallen?

"why is thy countenance fallen" = "heaven gave rain" = rain falls from heaven = fallen from grace = the fallen angel.

"inhabitants of the cities" = Fallen angel = "for it is the number of a man" = "and all the inhabitants of the cities" = "the city and the tower, which the children of men builded." = "for it is the number of a man; and his number is Six hundred threescore(60) and six(600+60+6)." = [Ezra 2:13 The children of Adonikam, six hundred sixty and six.]

["The children of Adonikam" = "the city and the tower, which the children of men builded."

Men = Adonikam = "Six days shalt thou labour = Suffer

Adonikam came with Zerubbabel from Babylon captivity = Civilization]

This is similar to what happened with Moses. Moses freed people from civilization or the taskmaster or the cult but some of the people already had the curse and the curse begets cursed so the "flock" was tainted. This is why Moses was angry in this comment.

[Exodus 32:19 And it came to pass, as soon as he came nigh unto the camp, that he saw the calf, and the dancing: and Moses' anger waxed hot, and he cast the tables out of his hands, and brake them beneath the mount.]

This is like a poisoned well. Moses and also Zerubbabel freed people from the cities but some of them had the curse and in turn they created more cursed or they spoke poorly of the "lord" . They took the Lords name in vain. The basically discredited the Lords and this created seeds of deceit and before long the people ignored the fear not remedy and started getting the written language education and did not apply the covenant , the remedy, fear not, suggested by Abraham and soon enough the curse was spreading again.

This is relative to when Socrates was in jail and his friend said I will pay the guards to let you go and you can escape and Socrates said something along the lines of "where can I go." This means there is no escape. There is nowhere to run to get away from the cursed.

"that he saw the calf, and the dancing: and Moses' anger waxed hot, and he cast the tables out of his hands, and brake them beneath the mount." = [2 Corinthians 4:9 Persecuted, but not forsaken; cast down, but not destroyed;} = cast down = trying to reached the ones cursed is essentially impossible because the curse is so powerful. = [Mark 15:34 And at the ninth hour Jesus cried with a loud voice, saying, Eloi, Eloi, lama sabachthani? which is, being interpreted, My God, my God, why hast thou forsaken me?] = "anger waxed hot" because he could not communicate with the cursed any better than Moses or Abraham. Because of this failure to communicate the only viable solution was = [Judges 8:17 And he beat down the tower of Penuel, and slew the men of the city.] = [Genesis 19:24 Then the LORD rained upon Sodom and upon Gomorrah brimstone and fire from the LORD out of heaven;

Genesis 19:25 And he overthrew those cities, and all the plain, and all the inhabitants of the cities, and that which grew upon the ground.] = "overthrew those cities, and all the plain, and all the inhabitants of the cities" = extermination of the cursed, and even using that extreme technique they still failed and this is an indication of how inviting or how good of a Trojan horse the curse is relative to = [Genesis 3:6

...saw that the tree was good for food, and that it was pleasant to the eyes, and a tree to be desired to make one wise,].

This is why the tree of knowledge is fatal to our species.= [Genesis 2:17 But of the tree of the knowledge of good and evil, thou shalt not eat of it: for in the day that thou eatest thereof thou shalt surely die.]
It is unstoppable or impossible to stop the spread of the "tree". Right brain loves impossibilities because it makes it think it has to try, and that's truly laughable.

This is the battle plan although you may not grasp it [Ezekiel 29:8 Therefore thus saith the Lord GOD; Behold, I will bring a sword upon thee, and cut off man and beast out of thee.]
"cut off man and beast out of thee" = Apply the fear not remedy = exorcism and that if doesn't work there is always plan A = [Judges 8:17 And he beat down the tower of Penuel, and slew the men of the city.] = [Genesis 19:24 Then the LORD rained upon Sodom and upon Gomorrah brimstone and fire from the LORD out of heaven; Genesis 19:25 And he overthrew those cities, and all the plain, and all the inhabitants of the cities, and that which grew upon the ground.] = "slew the men of the city."

I am infinitely open minded to all plans. The cursed continue to curse the youth because they do not know how to apply the written language education properly so that the education does not leave the children mentally crippled, mar sin féin mé díreach mar an cursed seo a dhéanamh do leanaí, siad a thuilleadh ar mian leo breathe. Cé a bhfuil le rá agat orm?- 6:16:11 AM

Compassion, mercy and patience do not apply when dealing with a person or group of people that mentally cripples an innocent child knowingly or unknowingly.

"...for I have sworn upon the altar of god eternal hostility against every form of tyranny over the mind of man." –*Thomas Jefferson to Benjamin Rush, 23 Sept. 1800*

They attack the truth in groups of three
The groups of three believe they see

Their numbers make them feel so right
Although three blind have no sight

One is say "That is not so" and two and three will say "We know."
One will say "You are so wrong" and two and three will sing his song.

They are wise in groups of three but still cannot find the door.
They are wise in groups of three but not as wise as the sea.

Because as one they cannot think, they need the group, they need the drink.
They believe their numbers makes them right, yet that is proof they have no sight.

[Mark 15:34 And at the ninth hour Jesus cried with a loud voice, saying, Eloi, Eloi, lama sabachthani? which is, being interpreted, My God, my God, why hast thou forsaken me?]
God did not forsake him it is just the curse is the son of a whore. The first reality of the battle is to not panic when you understand impossibility is before you. The curse is impossible to defeat so one has to understand how to defeat impossibility. Impossibility is defeated when a person starts seeing impossibility as possibility. One has to use the curse against itself. One has to turn the curse into a blessing and this requires thought. - 9:29:30 AM

Impossibility which is what the curse is defeats one because one tries to defeat it. To defeat impossibility one cannot try. The reason for this is impossibility will tire you out if you try and then you will be defeated. For this reason one has to not try to defeat the curse because the curse is impossible to defeat. What this "do not try" means is no rules, no morals and thus no barriers. If one clings to morals and barriers and rules those rules and morals and barriers will fall back on them and defeat them.

The curse has no rules or morals or barriers so one has to level the playing field by letting go of rules or morals or barriers as well. One has to be everything to be able to deal with anything and the only way one can be in that position is to be in a state of nothing or neutral. One has to mimic the curse in order to defeat the curse. Once one breaks the curse fully by applying the remedy, they have an advantage because they fully understand the curse and also how the cursed operate.

This strategy is similar to how a vaccine works. A vaccine is a virus that is dead so it is not harmful yet the body still sees it as a virus that is harmful so the body fights it off and creates antibodies so when the harmful live virus attacks the body is ready for it.

The cursed are far too great in number to wage actual physical battle against. The cursed do have some weaknesses. One weakness is freedom of speech and freedom of press. What this means is one is going to have to apply the remedy and then become a master of words. This is relative mimicking the curse. Use words which are the curse against the curse. Words are more effective in the battle against the curse because words can go places one physically cannot go. One has to get very good at the art of disguise relative to having explanations that fit into all aspects of knowledge relative to the cursed. One is going to have to have an airtight explanation whether they are speaking to Christians or Buddhists or Hindu's or Muslims or Jews or Atheists or Pagans or Scientists or Physicians or Psychologists or their own relatives or their next door neighbor or the depressed or the drug addicted or the prostitute.

One is going to have to concede they are unable to tell which of these groups is going to be welcoming on any given day to what one suggest about the curse. The bottom line is, any human being who got this education and did not apply the remedy to the full measure is cursed. That is universal. The cursed beget cursed.

The cursed are in this dark state of mind and they are in groups and when you start to talk to them one of them may start to understand you but their friends will quickly mock you and tell you to shut up because the darkness likes company and hates itself so it cannot stand to be alone.

One is going to have to be a smooth talker without morals. What this means is one is going to get defeated 100% of the time but they are not going to feel it is a loss. One will be defeated 100% of the time so one is going to love defeat and that will turn that curse into a blessing. Simply put, one is never going to lose because one is never going to win.

There are many ways to tell if one breaks the curse but the most obvious and easy to tell is when one loses sense of time. The mark of the beast/curse is [Galatians 4:10 Ye observe days, and months, and times, and years.] and so one knows they broke the curse or lost the mark when their mind no longer senses or registers time. This is not about saying the word time or saying the word day, this is relative to the mind itself no longer registers time at all. If one senses time at all they need to apply the remedy still. This is relative to going the full measure. Cold is one who has strong sense of time, lukewarm is one who has some sense of time and hot is one who has no sense of time.

There is a great paradox when dealing with the cursed.
One should communicate with the cursed.
One should not communicate with the cursed.

One should communicate with the cursed:
The cursed are your friends and are of your species and so they are your friends they are just cursed and only you can assist them to break the curse once you break the curse. That is why you should communicate with them. They are simply a friend on the road in need of some assistance so you are going to be a good Samaritan and assist them to break the curse and once you apply the remedy and break the curse you will understand that is what your life purpose is going to be.

One should not communicate with the cursed:
When one is in neutral they can read anyone they speak with so when they communicate with the sane they read the sane and mimic the sane and thus the curse, so they cannot take too much of dealing with the sane before the curse of the sane begins to harm them.
So the paradox is one who has broken the curse has to communicate with the sane to assist them to break the curse but in doing this they feel the curse and it harms them, so it's quite a dance.

One has to feel the curse that is of the sane in order to help the sane break the curse.

After one breaks the curse they will speak to the sane and after a short while the sane will start asking questions and coming to sequential conclusions and will confuse you. What is really happening is one starts to be confused like the sane because on is mimicking the sane. One is actually telepathically reading the sane and the sane are cursed and thus confused so one becomes confused also. This is why many of these wise beings spoke. Like the sermon on the mount for example. The sermon on the mount was not a question and answer forum it was a sermon or a teaching because once the sane start asking questions the speaker will become confused because they can read the ones asking questions.

Simply put once one breaks the curse of mental hell they have to go back to mental hell they broke free from to try and assist others break their mental hell. By "have to" I mean, ones intuition will not allow one to see their friends suffer and turn a blind eye to it and one will be rewarded by being mocked and told they are insane and perhaps even killed by the sane if one is worth their salt.

[Luke 12:4 And I say unto you my friends, Be not afraid of them that kill the body, and after that have no more that they can do.]

"Be not afraid of them that kill the body" = " Be not afraid" =[Genesis 15:1 … Fear not,] = [John 15:13 Greater love hath no man than this, that a man lay down his life for his friends.]

Friends = the ones who have the curse are your friends because they are of your species and you would want them to assist you to break the curse if they broke it, but since they are cursed they may end up killing for trying to assist them to break the curse. So accept the reality you are going to get your teeth kicked down your throat on a daily basis. You are dealing with the curse and the curse has your friends.

[John 15:13 Greater love hath no man than this, that a man lay down his life for his friends.]

.- 3:23:58 PM

The Sane - http://www.youtube.com/watch?v=sF5T844DVy4

Indifference is required when seeking victory in the face of impossibility.

91

4:54:30 PM – This is relative to the concept of disciples. Once you apply the remedy the full measure and break the curse the ones you know before you break the curse are not going to believe you did break the curse or believe what you say.

Buddha broke the curse and returned to his wife and children and then left them. Jesus broke the curse but his mother and father did not believe him or they would have been his disciples. The reason for this is because breaking the curse is a mental reality and so ones who are physical based mentally and are still cursed cannot grasp it easily. Ones who knew Jesus before he broke the curse, his mother and father, did not see a huge difference other than the fact he spoke differently. This is the same with Buddha. This is why Moses suggested honor your father and mother because he knew the ones you know before you break the curse will not believe it.

This is why some go to Temples and leave their family and their friends after they break the curse. I am far too stupid to do that because I like the hot coals. I am aware I will never convince anyone who knew me before the accident to apply the remedy. Jesus explains how he met the fisherman and they threw down their nets and applied the remedy. This suggests Jesus did not know them. This reality is a strange thing because it would seem the people you have known all your life would certainly believe you and apply the remedy but it is in fact just the reverse. This is not suggesting it's easy to convince ones you did not know before you apply the remedy. I am zero for six billion in relation to convincing anyone to apply the remedy but I understand I am zero for six billion so I have gained an understanding. The fact these wise beings had even one disciple, meaning ones who they convinced to apply the remedy, is proof of impossibility based on its own merits.

This single comment is impossibility : [Luke 17:33 ;and whosoever shall lose his life shall preserve it.]

X = state of mind after the education : extreme left brain state of mind = Ego

Y = State of mind after one applies the remedy = No Ego= sound mind left and right brain working equally

So, and whosoever shall lose his life(X) shall preserve it(Y).

92

That is simply impossibility and I accomplished it by accident so I am not even saying I could do it intentionally. I am not even certain it can be done intentionally and that is an indication of how powerful the curse is. This is why it is important after you break the curse to let go of morals because you are going to lose so often you will talk yourself into giving up. There is no such thing as three strikes you are out in this battle. One fights until they drop and by that time maybe you will convince one person to apply the remedy and that will mean you accomplished the impossible but did not really make a dent in the war.

If all one had to do was the impossible to win the war it would have been won 5000 years ago. This means the war itself is harder than impossible and that is an indication of how strong the curse is. Written language has been around over 5400 years and in that time there has not been one person who broke the curse of written language that has convinced the species written language has some pretty bad mental side effects if not applied properly. This is an indication of how powerful this tree of knowledge curse is. This curse is so powerful it makes people hallucinate and sense time. It makes people afraid of words. It makes people kill their self over money. It makes people sacrifice their own first born to it.

There are some drugs that people take, recreational drugs, and their sense of time is reduced. So people take these drugs and their sense of time is reduced or time goes very slowly. This is an indication that the strong sense of time one feels when not on those drugs is false because it can be altered. The problem is with drugs one will harm their self trying to maintain this mental state.

So the drugs unveiled the right brain a bit and then the person loses their sense of time a bit but in order to maintain that they harm their self with the drugs. When a person has the curse slight sense of time is attractive because they have such a strong sense of time when "sober".

So the drugs will unveil right brain for the duration that drug lasts but it will harm that person eventually trying to maintain that feeling. Feeling mental euphoria from drugs is a symptom one is still cursed. This is why Jesus made this comment [Ephesians 5:18 And be not drunk with wine, wherein is excess; but be filled with the Spirit;] because he was trying to explain that drugs are not bad but they may harm you and you can get the exact same euphoria if you break the curse by doing this :

X = state of mind after the education : extreme left brain state of mind = Ego

Y = State of mind after one applies the remedy = No Ego= sound mind left and right brain working equally

and whosoever shall lose his life(X) shall preserve it(Y).

"Spirit" = right brain = unveiled right brain = left and right brain are equally active.

"Spirit of fear" = left brain extreme = hypothalamus not working properly= [2 Timothy 1:7 For God hath not given us the spirit of fear; but of power, and of love, and of a sound mind.]

Spirit = sound mind = no fear

Spirit of fear = unsound mind = fearful=[Galatians 4:10 Ye observe days, and months, and times, and years.]= strong sense of time = suffering

I wasn't ready to wake up in fact I was attempting to check out but once the remedy is applied right brain will start powering up and it is so powerful you are kind of along for the ride for the first ten months or so. One will have to get use to how powerful it is. It is a shock to the system because one is going from unsound mind, extreme left brain, to sound mind and unveiling right brain is not like unveiling another left brain, right brain is subconscious when you are in extreme left brain so it's like adding shuttle booster rockets to a moped. Because of this it is a shock to the system and that means for the first month or so one is going to be mentally incapacitated. This is because the mind itself has been in this sequential left brain state for so long when this turbo charger kicks in the mind has to get use to it. The is because when a person is a child they get the sequential conditioning before right brain even gets a chance to get started so a person never even feels right brain at full strength before it is veiled by the education.

[Matthew 19:14 But Jesus said, Suffer little children, and forbid them not, to come unto me: for of such is the kingdom of heaven.]

Suffer the little children is why this happened = [Judges 8:17 And he beat down the tower of Penuel, and slew the men of the city.]

I understand Jesus was not as concerned about the adults who had the curse, he was more concerned with the children who the cursed where going to curse. Socrates was in fact killed for corrupting the minds of the youth. I understand he was trying to explain to them the problem of the education. The line in the sand is this. You got the education so you are cursed and that is your business but when you are complicit knowingly or unknowing in cursing the children because your educators do not know how to apply the education without mentally cursing the children there is only going to be this = "and slew the men of the city."

You put this curse on children and the fact I am certain that is what you are doing to them I have to stop you. I have to stop you even if it costs me my life. No one in history has stopped you even though it costs them their life trying to stop you. I do not mind repeat performances.

"…for I have sworn upon the altar of god eternal hostility against every form of tyranny over the mind of man." –*Thomas Jefferson to Benjamin Rush, 23 Sept. 1800*

I may certainly fail in stopping you, and I may certainly be killed in attempting to stop you.
[Luke 17:25 But first must he suffer many things, and be rejected of this generation.]
I am pleased I am beyond your understanding. Past is now.- 6:16:55 PM

Creativity is essential when dealing with rabidity.

10/17/2009 6:47:40 AM – It is important one understands I am not suggesting I am not cursed. I am suggesting I traded one aspect of the curse for another aspect accidentally.
In the extreme left brain state I had many emotions and fears and strong sense of time so it was suffering. Now I accidentally broke that curse I am cursed because I am aware of the curse and I cannot convince the ones who are under the suffering aspect of the curse they can achieve the aspect of the curse where there is no suffering.

Curse 1 = left brain extreme strong emotions strong sense of time and suffering.
Curse 2 = no emotions no sense of time and so one is indifferent so no suffering.

This is talking about ones in Curse 1.
[2 Peter 2:12 But these, as natural brute beasts, made to be taken and destroyed, speak evil of the things that they understand not; and shall utterly perish in their own corruption;]

"speak evil of the things that they understand not" = they hear but do not understand. Notice how this comment is out of sequence, in random access. It should be speak evil of things they do not understand.

This is suggesting Curse 2.
[Mark 8:21 And he said unto them, How is it that ye do not understand?]
So ones who break curse 1 get curse 2 and that is they cannot communicate with the ones in curse 1 and that is a curse also, but they are indifferent and do not suffer even though they are compelled to try to assist ones in curse 1 to wake up they cannot do it, and that is curse 2.
None of these wise beings convinced the species in any meaningful lasting way to break curse 1.
All I am suggesting is I do not suffer now like I did in curse 1 because I am in the machine state which is curse 2. This is how strong the curse is. We as a species fell from grace so one can be in level 1 curse or level 2 curse but the curse is everywhere. If one does not understand that or believe that then they are in curse 1 which is ignorance to the curse all together, they are wandering aimlessly. In curse 1 one has strong emotions so they get their feelings hurt easily and so they can give up easily. For example they might write a book or make a song or push an idea and people might say "I do not like that." and so they will give up. In curse 2 one has no ability to be insulted so they are immune to judgments of others so they just do and they are not even capable of being insulted.

These books I write are a nightmare in literary terms but I cannot feel what I should feel like with that understanding. What should I feel like knowing ones who thrive on this demotic invention will be displeased with my words? I am indifferent totally to their judgments. It does not matter if six billion people say "You should give up in writing books because they all suck." I am writing infinite books into infinity and no comment by anyone is going to make any difference to that reality.

I am mindful they are in curse 1 so why would I pay any heed to them.

[Luke 24:45 Then opened he their understanding, that they might understand the scriptures,}

The ones in curse 1 understandings are not open, or they still have right brain veiled so they know not what they do or say. A better way to look at it is:

[2 Corinthians 11:19 For ye suffer fools gladly, seeing ye yourselves are wise.]

I am not concerned what a fool thinks about anything. A fool may insult me into infinity and I will not even acknowledge them and they will think I am pig headed or stupid because they cannot grasp I do not even see them at all. I do not listen to the words of fools. I humor myself by pretending I listen to the words of fools. The fools wish their judgments of me worked. The fools judgments of other fools work so they assume their judgments of me will work and that is their greatest delusion. This time around I have freedom of speech and freedom of press and if any fool gets in the way of that they better have their death shroud on. Simply put, you leave me be, and I will consider leaving you be, and stop insulting the wise beings because if you were capable of detecting wisdom I would remind you.- 7:13:36 AM

[Luke 24:45 Then opened he their understanding, that they might understand the scriptures,]

So this comment is an attempt to explain one in extreme left brain only see's parts so when that person reads these ancient texts they come to a different understanding about them than a person who unveils right brain comes to because when right brain is unveiled, curse 1 is broken, they get the spirit or see the whole of these ancient texts.

"Then opened he their understanding" this is also a sentence in random access, right brain. It should be "Then he opened their understanding". So if this being said this sentence to you today you would say " What drugs are you on?" and he would say [Acts 2:15 For these are not drunken, as ye suppose, seeing it is but the third hour of the day.] and you would say "You are crazy and need medical help and probably should be killed because you cannot even speak the language properly so you certainly are crazy or evil because you are not like me." An that is serving the serpent. Every time you insult a person for misspelling a word you do the bidding of the serpent and in turn that is your god. You should call your cult leader and ask him if that is true because that is infinitely over your head.

The only reason I would never say you need medical help is because there is no drug in the dam universe that can help you with your extreme hallucination neurosis. There is no drug and there is no prayer that can help you because you are cursed above all cattle [Genesis 3:14 And the LORD God said unto the serpent(you), Because thou hast done this(got the written language ,demotic education), thou art cursed above all cattle(you), and above every beast of the field(you); upon thy belly shalt thou go(you), and dust shalt thou eat all the days of thy life(you):]

It is not important what your cult leader says contrary to that because if they were capable of any wisdom ever into infinity I would remind you. Do you know of any drugs or prayers that can cure this "thou art cursed above all cattle" because if you think you do, it proves you are cursed above all cattle. There is only one remedy and you will never pull it off because you run from the remedy back into the curse because you are cursed above all cattle. I am not concerned what your cult leader tells you after he takes all your money.

[Luke 17:33 ;and whosoever shall lose his life shall preserve it.]
X = state of mind after the education: extreme left brain state of mind = Ego

Y = State of mind after one applies the remedy = No Ego= sound mind left and right brain working equally
So, and whosoever shall lose his life(X) shall preserve it(Y).

If you choose not to apply the remedy, do not ever complain. Do not ever whine. Do not ever get around children because you are the serpent. Do not ever pass a law because you are not capable of making a judgment at all. Here is what you think about everything I say because you see truth as lies because you are the serpent.
<KarenJ> Lestat I perceive you are mentally ill and need help very badly.

So when this is said [Luke 24:45 Then opened he their understanding,] which is in random access, right brain you say, <KarenJ> Lestat I perceive you are mentally ill and need help very badly. Then I say [Acts 2:15 For these are not drunken, as ye suppose, seeing it is but the third hour of the day.]

It is almost as if I can't talk freely because I upset the little mentally cursed one when I speak freely. I am not looking for acceptance from a mentally cursed being that is so mentally cursed they do this: =[Galatians 4:10 Ye observe days, and months, and times, and years.]

Although you are cursed above all cattle and although the adults you trusted cursed you above all cattle that doesn't change the fact I cannot help you. I cannot even reach you because when I try to associate with you, your curse harms me. Your curse is so strong it bleeds into me if I associate with you or try to communicate with you to assist you to break the curse. You are so cursed everything around you becomes cursed and when I tell you that you say: <KarenJ> Lestat I perceive you are mentally ill and need help very badly.

And what is even more devastating is when you say that to me you perceive correctly because you only see truth as lies and only see light as darkness. You see me as the serpent because you are the serpent. I see you as perfection but I have to deny that because I see everything as one thing and that is not true. I see you as perfection with a curse that can be broken but the very nature of the curse mean's you do not want to walk through the door to break the curse because the curse makes you see the door as a wall.

I would like to help you but the curse is far too strong. It is just too strong. I cannot defeat the curse and no one else has either in all of recorded history. All these wise beings tried to defeat the curse but at the end of the day the curse remains. The adults are still sacrificing their first born offspring to demotic so everything the wise beings did was not enough. If the wise beings did not say one word about the curse it would not have made any difference because the curse is so powerful it is impossibility.

We as a species have started a curse than cannot be stopped. Once in a while someone breaks the curse of demotic but then they gain the curse of failure to communicate with the cursed of demotic. The curse is perfect so only a person who doesn't try to break the curse can break it fully and achieve curse 2 status, perhaps, the least among you. The least of the least is the only one that can break the curse and that is what is known as meek.

The curse is so air tight only an accident can break the curse fully but that is relative to that person who has the accident not relative to the curse on a world scale or a species scale. The curse is like a virus that is out of hand and is so far out of hand there is no recovery from it now. One can try to have a positive outlook but that is all shattered when one realizes the curse is caused by teaching children written language without any regards for what this sequential based left brain education will do to a child's mind if there is no random access education employed equally with it.

The species as a whole does not even believe 12 years of sequential based, left brain education could possibly harm a child's mind. The society as a whole believes it actually makes a child wise. I do not even bother quoting people who understand the brain and the mind and totally agree with the spirit of what I suggest because you are cursed and nothing will make you believe what I say is truth. I can walk on water and you still will not believe written language creates major mental side effects. I can turn sticks into snakes and you still will not believe written language creates the curse. I can move heaven and earth and you will still not believe written language creates the curse.

You believe written language could not have any bad side effects because someone told you it does not have any bad side effects. So here is exactly what you believe about written language.

[Genesis 3:6 ... saw that the tree was good for food, and that it was pleasant to the eyes, and a tree to be desired to make one wise,..]

You look at something that destroys a child's mind if not applied properly and you say to yourself "I want to give that to my child." So never speak about how you care about the children because I understand you are a mental rapist of innocent children.

"...for I have sworn upon the altar of god eternal hostility against every form of tyranny

over the mind of man." –*Thomas Jefferson to Benjamin Rush, 23 Sept. 1800* - 8:54:51 AM

11:46:08 AM – I woke up today around 6AM and now it is 11:46 AM and I have spit blood in my books and hung myself about a billion times with my words in that span of time but my mind is telling me it has been about 1000 years in that span of time. One day is like 1000 years is actually quite reserved in explaining no sense of time. The best way to look at no sense of time is just infinity. It is just simply infinity and there is no mental sensation of time passing because one is mentally in the now at all times.

So these clocks I look at are simply so I can be reminded I no longer notice time at all in any respect at all. The thing about nirvana is you cannot get out of it so you do not panic because you have no emotions to feel panic so you are just indifferent to it all together. At times I think I get use to it but its nothingness so you tend to feel everything at select moments so you can't get use to it because it is nothingness and one can't get use to nothing yet one is unable to feel sad or happy so it's really what limbo is explained to be like.

I cannot explain what it is like in infinite books but there is no reason I should not try to explain it because all I have is infinity. I am really not angry with anyone I am simply trying to get use to no sense of time. I am trying many different methods and none of them work. I have job security. I am unable to tell if applying this fear not remedy to break the curse is good or bad because if I could tell that I would not be in nirvana. Another way to look at it is right brain has ambiguity so I have lots of doubt and I will suggest you should apply the remedy and then suggest you should not because right brain also has lots of paradox which is contradictions. One has to feel what it is like to not be happy or sad but be right in the middle of those two feelings and that is nirvana or neutral.

I can no longer relate to people who are always happy or always sad because I have my emotions purged so I cannot even relate to what happy or sad felt like when I did experience those emotions before the accident. Nothingness is a very accurate description but I think neutral state of mind is a better way to describe it because on average one is neutral.

What is odd is usually a person reaches nirvana or at least part way to nirvana with the help of a teacher. This teacher assists that one in the ways of nirvana so to speak. When one reaches nirvana by accident they have no teacher and no teacher can help them because they already reached nirvana. So for example Jesus reached nirvana and then he taught his disciples the ways of nirvana. Buddha reached nirvana and then he taught his disciples the ways of nirvana but no one taught Jesus or Buddha the ways of nirvana because they reached it on their own or by accident. The big fish so to speak don't' have teachers or didn't have teachers because they are the teacher.

I tend to scare everyone away so I am a poor teacher because I am uncertain if anyone should want to reach nirvana because I have lots of ambiguity or doubt. I have moments of doubt about nirvana. I understand I do not want to trick anyone. I am mindful to explain both sides of the coin and that is required so I can keep writing into infinity. I do not have a bottom line argument because then the argument may stop. Perhaps the written language alters the mind perhaps and perhaps fear not is the remedy perhaps. That is a very safe comment so if you get anything out of all my infinite books just read that last sentence.- 12:11:11 PM

These are supposed to be Doc Holidays last words "Well I'll be damned. This is funny."
Even if they are not his last words they explain things fairly well.
Voltaire on his death bed was asked by a Priest to renounce Satan and Voltaire replied, "Now, now, my good man, this is no time for

making enemies." He didn't want to renounce that Priest in his final moments.
- 1:24:58 PM

3:16:33 PM – I went out to eat and saw people and they all looked perfect to me so I am doomed.

"A witty saying proves nothing."
<u>Voltaire</u>
Sounds are intangible but can produce tangible results when arranged properly.
A quick witted response usually indicates one is confused.

11:34:21 PM – I am mindful I am talking a lot about ancient texts. I am mindful many assume I am religious or a philosopher or some other sort of guru or sorcerer. I am not, I am an accident.
I opened my understandings accidentally and now I am testing their limits. I understand things you do not understand and I understand them by accident.

I am not capable of feeling loss or sorrow or prolonged anger or bitterness but I do not want anyone to think I am a holy roller because then the sane will turn me and my words into a money making opportunity. I am mindful I fail if they turn me into a money making opportunity.

I am not capable of being angry or happy because I am in neutral but it is important I try to explain what I try to remember about the forty years before the accident. I was shy. I was embarrassed easily. I was afraid of the dark. I thought I was dumb because I didn't make A's in school. By high school I was ruined mentally from the many years of sequential education. I recall the people I knew in school who got all A's were very quiet and shy and they kept to their self. I remember one girl and she got all A's on everything and she would never talk to anyone and she was very shy and very reserved and now I understand that's a trend. The ones who get all A's and B's are conditioned way too far to the left and they tend to break mentally eventually.

They tend to snap eventually. Of course everyone who gets this education snaps in one way or another. The problem is everyone learns how to read and everyone learns how to write and everyone learns math to a degree and once that is done the mind is conditioned all the way to the left. The mind is so far to the left the person senses time and the emotions are so strong the person is ready to snap at any minute.

I gave up on life at about 24. I was judged to not be intelligent enough to get into college by judges of intelligence.

What you call civilization or the civilized have an infinite problem now. One might suggest the tables have turned. I could have easily died because you assumed your written language education had no bad side effects on the mind even though you know it's all sequential based and many beings in society who understand the mind have told you there is not enough right brain education in the education system.

They tried to warn you and now it is too late for you. I understand you cannot pay me back for what you did to me so I am going to pay you back for what you did to me. Do unto others as you would have them do unto you. Isto significa que quere morrer porque me puxo nun estado de metal que me fixo querer morrer. Eu quero que vostede sabe que podo entender que quere morrer.

A N (21) took her life one month after her father also killed himself

These two people want me to let you know they understand you want to die, eye for an eye.

I understand I could be in the ground right now because or your assumptions of how to teach wisdom but I am not in the ground, but you will be in the ground. Do you think I am emotional or are you hallucinating out of your damned mind?

You do not have enough money, and there is not enough money in the infinite universe to compensate me for what you did to me, so I am going to take your head and call it even. Do you think I am emotional or are you hallucinating out of your damned mind?

I am not here to reason with you. I am not here to make peace with you. I am here to silence you. Are you hallucinating out of your damned mind or do you just believe words to the point you will kill because of them? Block your emotions.

I will tell you how I was about a week before the final suicide attempt. I was mindful about my life and I was thinking back on all the things I perceived went wrong. I thought if I got into college my life would have been great. I thought if I would have joined the military after not getting into college my life would have been great. I thought maybe I should have married at a young age and had kids and my life would have been great. I kept thinking these thoughts that final week until I was sick to my stomach with depression. I was no longer sad I was physically sick. My body was sick and it felt like my stomach was in a knot and I could not even stand to be alive for another moment. There are some who say one should let the past go. I do not care what a mental rapist of children think about anything because their death cannot come too soon.

I do not care if there are six billion of them, I spit in their face. The reality about the sane is they do very bad things and then they figure it out way after the fact, and then they kind of go hide somewhere and no one answers for the deed. But now the tables have turned.

I am living proof civilization is a mental rapist of children and civilization is far too stupid to understand that I woke up from the mental death they put me in with their wisdom education.

About a year ago I took a handful of pills to escape what I thought was my failed life and when I started to convulse I decided I wanted to die, and somehow I did not die, and now I am aware of why I took those pills, and it was because civilization conditioned me so far into left brain with their wisdom education that I was hallucinating that civilization should be listened to at all. Who are you to me? Do you think your longevity is increasing or decreasing? Do you understand history repeats itself?

[Judges 8:17 And he beat down the tower of Penuel, and slew the men of the city.]

Do you think I am emotional or are you hallucinating out of your damned mind? Let's see what the wise beings would have done.

[Genesis 18:26 And the LORD said, If I find in Sodom fifty righteous within the city, then I will spare all the place for their sakes.]

105

Well there might be fifty.

[Genesis 18:29 And he spake unto him yet again, and said, Peradventure there shall be forty found there. And he said, I will not do it for forty's sake.]

I won't spare the city for forty though and based on my chat room experiences there isn't even twenty. That's not good news for you.

What civilization did to you mentally with their wisdom education because it was not applied properly was so devastating you cannot even tell how mentally ruined you are. I certainly could not tell, I just thought I was dumb and depressed because teachers said I was dumb with their report cards of judgment based on tests of one's ability to think sequentially.

[Genesis 19:11 And they smote the men that were at the door of the house with blindness, both small and great: so that they wearied themselves to find the door.]

You are so mentally blind you cannot find the door out of the hell you are mentally in. I will say that again because you are so mentally blind you cannot even understand anything I say ever. You are so mentally blind you cannot find the door out of the hell you are mentally in. You cannot get out of mental hell because you cannot even see the door.

I am telling you I accidentally broke the curse and I am telling you your sense of time is proof you are cursed and you will go ask your cult leader if that is true because you cannot think for yourself any longer. You cannot see the door out of the mental hell you are in and your cult leader cannot see the door out of the mental hell you are in either because you are both blind because you are cursed with mental blindness.

Do my run on sentences please you or do they drive you mad? I ponder why I even write these books. I am compelled to write them but I am not sure where they even go. There are many human beings on this planet who are awake to a degree and have broken the curse to a degree and they find no fault with what I write in spirit in my books. Between you and me I do not remember what I write in my books exactly but I have a general spirit of what I write about in my mind. Relative to me I am just saying the same thing over and over and over. Perhaps I am in over and over and over psychosis. - 10/18/2009 1:01:11 AM

"One is very crazy when in love."
Sigmund Freud

Love opens all the doors better left shut.
Love is simply attachment in disguise.
Whatever one loves they hate when it is gone and loving to hate is insanity.
Love fills all the gaps that should be filled with wisdom.
If one loves their self they are arrogant and if they love someone else they idolize.
Love is fleeting so lovers are searching for it.
Love is fleeting so trying to catch love only leads to suffering.
Love is a river that ends at a waterfall.
One cannot love what they do not own so love is simply an attempt at control.
Love; attachment; suffering; hate.

10:18:09 AM – [Revelation 17:16 And the ten horns which thou sawest upon the beast, these shall hate the whore, and shall make her desolate and naked, and shall eat her flesh, and burn her with fire.]

Let's get on with making her desolate and naked.
    What is a language teacher? I will use the word English. An English teacher is a judge. This judge makes sure a student gets the sequential aspects of written language down or they are judged unfavorably.
Spelling is simply arranging letters in proper sequence.
    Catt or Cta is not proper sequence so a teacher would judge that a failure and tell a student cat is the proper spelling. So a teacher is this judge that rewards a student on how well they sequence and sequence is left brained so a teacher judges a student on how well they condition their self into left brain. Students who condition their self into left brain well are rewarded and students who do not are punished with bad grades from the judge.

The bad grades from the judge are taken home to the parents and the parents judge the student and perhaps punish or threaten the student with punishment. So the teacher judge and the parent judge threaten the student using fear tactics or threats of punishment so the child will condition their self in extreme left brain. So a student does not have any choice but to condition their self because the teacher and the parents are threatening them with punishment if they do not condition their self into left brain.

So a parent will tell a student or child, "Go up to your room and condition yourself into left brain and then you can go outside and play." Or will say "Is all of your left brain conditioning finished?" The parent and teacher will call it homework but really it is simply they are making the child not only condition their self at school they want to condition them when they are home also. They do not want to do anything but condition that child as far into sequential left brain as possible as quickly as possible. This why the children are mentally conditioned all the way into left brain before the age of 8 or 9 and the bad side effects start showing up at around the age of 12 or 14.

Sentence structure is simply arranging words in proper sequence.
So a student might write:
[Luke 24:45 Then opened he their understanding,...]
And the teacher judge would say "No that is wrong or bad, it should be 'Then he opened their understanding.'" The reality is the English teacher judge is not a teacher it is a judge against right brain. The society hires this person to make sure all the students get conditioned into left brain and in turn silences the complex right brain. This makes them nice and dumb and makes them prone to fear tactics. The students are easier to control when they cannot think for their self.

The parents are more willing to allow their children to be conditioned into extreme brain when there are perceived rewards attached to the conditioning. The logic is, without education one will not make money and they will have a difficult life. The truth is one is going to have a difficult life if they veil their right brain as a result of getting the education or having the education applied improperly.

So society or civilization as a whole hates right brain. If a student spells the word out of sequence they get punish and if they arrange a sentence out of sequenced based on the teachers judgment of what is proper or improper and that is based on what another person has judged is improper or proper then the child is punished. Who taught that teacher? Another teacher. Who taught that teachers teacher? Another teacher. Who is thinking for their self? No one is, they are sheep doing as they have been told and that is good because they cannot think for their self any way.

They cannot think for their self because their mind has been veiled and that is because of the education so the term the blind leading the blind is what is really happening. So the entire education system is based on English and math and both are all about sequencing and getting things in proper sequence based on rules and all this does is condition one into extreme left brain and it will never create a wise student because it ruins their mind.

All education creates are mentally unsound beings, extreme left brain, who are very prone to fear tactics and are hallucinating to the point they sense time and all their emotions are turned up so high they are nervous wrecks. In fact you are so mentally unsound you sense time. Why don't you go ask your cult leader if that is truth so they can tell you what to think. - 10:54:02 AM

[[Revelation 17:16 And the ten horns which thou sawest upon the beast, these shall hate the whore, and shall make her desolate and naked, and shall eat her flesh, and burn her with fire.]
I eat the whore's demotic flesh for no reason and I beg you to stop me. That certainly blew it.

12:38:13 AM – Don't mind that above entry I am simply pondering if I should allow you to live.
You go ahead and pray to your whore demotic that I achieve infinite mercy and compassion.

10/19/2009 6:28:34 AM – There are only 2 great truths in all the universe relative to human beings. The complexity of the two great truths is that they are interdependent. One cannot believe one or the other truth, they have to believe both truths or they will not believe either truth. The problem with the two great truths is they shatter illusions.

If one believes the two great truths their world as they perceive it starts to crumble and the problem with that is ones who have the curse, have their right brain veiled, and right brain has creativity so they cannot adapt and so they hate the two great truths because they are not capable of adapting to the two great truths. Simply put, if they believe the two great truths the vast majority of everything they have come to believe becomes lies and they cannot accept or adapt to that so they hate the two great truths.

The sane hate the two great truths and they hate anyone who speaks the two great truths. There are no exceptions to this. Once you apply the remedy you will speak of the two great truths and you are going to be mocked and hated and spit on by the sane. It is important you understand this upfront so you do not get discouraged. So the two great truths shatter the illusions of the sane and so they hate them and hate anyone who suggests them.

[1 John 3:13 Marvel not, my brethren, if the world hate you.]

The world is the sane because the sane number like the grains of sand in the sea and they control the world and thus are the world. They will hate you for suggesting the two great truths because they are in hallucination world to the point they sense time and they love their hallucination world and do not want to leave it.

Some may have told you that you can overcome any problem if you put your mind to it. That is not true. Once you break the curse you will understand there is a one problem you cannot overcome. This particular problem goes back 5400 years and perhaps 7000 years and no one has overcome it yet. No one has even come close to overcoming this problem just a lot of people got butchered for trying to overcome this problem.

The reason the sane hate when you suggest the two great truths and cannot believe the two great truths is because when it shatters their illusions and thus their world everything falls apart for them. Once one applies the remedy their outlook on everything reverses. Not on some things, on everything. That is why this comment was made.

[Luke 14:26 If any man come to me, and hate not his father, and mother, and wife, and children, and brethren, and sisters, yea, and his own life also, he cannot be my disciple.]

All this is saying is you have to hate your life and everything you call your life because after you get the curse what you call life is really death and that is why the remedy kills that.
[Luke 17:33 ;and whosoever shall lose his life shall preserve it.]
X = state of mind after the education: extreme left brain state of mind = Ego
Y = State of mind after one applies the remedy = No Ego= sound mind left and right brain working equally
So, and whosoever shall lose his life(X) shall preserve it(Y).

Simply put, after you get the education you are mentally dead and so in order to become mentally awake you have to kill that mental dead aspect and when you do that you are going to be aware all of these people you know are mentally dead also. After you break the curse you will understand who is cursed and you will not be able to reach them. This is why the sane hate the two great truths and hate anyone who suggests them.

The world of the sane shatters in the light of the two great truths. The sane have this mental state called pride and if they believed the two great truths their pride would destroy them so to avoid that they hate anyone who suggests the two great truths.

This is why relative to some religion/belief systems ones leave their family and break ties with everyone they ever knew. I do not do that because I applied the remedy accidentally and I love the hottest coals. I am a glutton for punishment. I will speak with people and tell them the two great truths and they will say right to my face "What you are saying is totally insane and no person who understands the norms of the world would agree with you so you are crazy." To me their comments are expected and I have no emotional capacity so I am not surprised because I understand I would not believe the two great truths either and I didn't believe them, I accidentally discovered them. So I do not marvel when they spit in my face.
[1 John 3:13 Marvel not, my brethren, if the world hate you.]

You may get the impression when you break the cursed the world gets easier but in reality when you break the curse you will understand the world is the mentally dead. You will break the curse and join the team that never wins and gets their teeth kicked in, but you will be in the machine state and you will be immune to their delusional judgments. The sane only see the truth as lies, they have no eyes.

One should not jump into supernatural until they can grasp elementary cause and effect relationships. If one substitutes the tree of knowledge, written language, for a hot stove and then someone says "Do not touch that hot stove it will burn you." One would not assume that is a supernatural warning because in fact it is just a cause and effect relationship.

If one gets twelve years of sequential left brain education and nearly no right brain random access education they are going to get mentally burned, and that is not supernatural that is an elementary cause and effect relationship. To me this is all so obvious but to the sane they only see lies because they are so attached to these things [[Luke 14:26 If any man come to me, and hate not his father, and mother, and wife, and children, and brethren, and sisters, yea, and his own life also, he cannot be my disciple.] they do not want to let go of them and mainly the last one, their life, because they do not understand their mental life is mental death. They love their neurosis and they are use to it and they cannot let go of it. - 7:36:16 AM

Exit - http://www.youtube.com/watch?v=9uaosgeJ29k

9:54:44 AM – The reality about the two greatest truths in the universe relative to human kind are so important to understand because if one does not understand them their house of understanding is upon the sand and so it crumbles easily. The two greatest truths are intertwined or if one does not grasp one of the truths they cannot grasp the other and thus their entire understanding of reality is in peril.

The two great truths rely on each other so they make up one great truth with two aspects, both aspects being equally important. The first great truth is what causes the curse and the second great truth is the remedy to the curse. If one does not believe the cause of the curse then they will not believe the remedy to the curse. If one does not believe the remedy to the curse they will not believe the cause of the curse, so they will remain cursed.

The power of the curse in part is it makes one who is cursed unable to see they are cursed and so the curse keeps the cursed blind to it. Sometimes when a person who has the curse does certain drugs their sense of time is diminished. Pot or drink is a good example, it slows ones sense of time down and that is a keystone that sense of time is a symptom of the curse. When one has the curse certain drugs make the curse apparent. One who is cursed will assume the drugs made their sense of time diminish but in reality the drugs reduces the effects of the curse. So when one is cursed and they are not on drugs, what they experience is the full effects of the curse and when they take drugs the effects of the curse are reduced and so there are people who take drugs often because they do not like the effects of the curse and rightly so but the drugs wear off so they have to do more and so they are harming their self to escape the harmful effects of the curse and that is part of the curse.

One does things that cause harm but they think it causes good. So they know not what they do. One who is cursed does drugs thinking they are escaping reality but their reality when sober is the curse so they end up harming their self trying to escape the curse they think is reality. The curse is not reality it is a hallucination because their mind is unsound so it is hallucinating.

So when one is cursed the drugs help them escape the strong effects of the curse so the drugs are a viable option to dealing with the curse but not a viable solution to the curse. That is what this comment means.

[Ephesians 5:18 And be not drunk with wine, wherein is excess; but be filled with the Spirit;]

Drugs are in excess because one can break the curse and feel the effect one feels when they are on drugs and one of those effects is no sense of time. Other effects are no stress, no nervousness, no embarrassment, no shyness, no hate, no anger, no bitterness, no self esteem issues. One is not going to be embarrassed or shy if they are drunk out of their mind but in order to maintain that state of mind they will harm their self by trying to remain drunk.

The drugs are not the problem they are simply one viable alternative to reducing the effects of the curse but there is a better way to reduce the effects of the curse and that is to eliminate or break the curse all together.

Once one breaks the curse they are not going to lose their sense of time on drugs because they will have no sense of time. One is not going to be less shy or less embarrassed on drugs because they will not be shy or embarrassed once they break the curse. So what would be the point of taking drugs if the drugs did not relieve the symptoms of the curse because the curse was broken? No point in doing drugs. It is not a matter of morals in relation to doing drugs or not. It is a simple reality that drugs will not work once the curse is broken.

A drug is simply a way to alter your perception but once the curse is broken, right brain is so powerful drugs cannot alter its perception so there is no point in doing drugs because they will not even make one feel any sort of euphoria because when right brain is unveiled or the curse is broken there are no drugs in the universe that can complete with that right brain perception or power.

The drugs only work from a euphoria aspect if one is cursed. This brings about a greater pondering because if everyone breaks the curse the drug trade or industry including alcohol will evaporate. There is no person who has a monetary vested interest in this drug trade that would want everyone to apply the remedy to the curse because they would lose all their money. The deeper reality is does a government want the people to be wiser than they are? Certainly not.

If the people were wiser than the government then there would be no need for the government. So the wiser the government appears to the people the more powerful the government is to the people. The government can only pull fast ones over on dumb people not wise people so it is the government's goal to keep the people as dumb as possible. Relative to the government the dumber the people are the easier they are to manipulate. One cannot be any dumber than they are after 12 years of hardcore sequential education called school.

First off left brain is sequential based and it is the dumber of the two aspects so education conditions one all the way into left brain so they cannot be any dumber after the education because the ones who teach it do not even have any right brain random access classes to counter act all the sequential based left brain classes.

If the education system had equal amounts of left and right brain education the people would be intelligent and wise and they would not be able to be taken advantage of and they would not be prone to fear tactics. That's not a good thing for the sheep because the sheep might start thinking for their self and that is a nightmare to a slave master. If the sheep all run off and start thinking for their self the slave master is doomed.

A slave master always wants more power and thus control and never wants to lose control or give up power. So to think the slave master is going to apply equal left and right brain education in the schools is a delusion because that would mean the slave master wants to give up power or control. This is why these wise beings were slaughtered wholesale. The task master will let many things slide but will never let his power and control slide. One has to understand the right hemisphere of their brain is theirs and it is theirs alone and it has been turned off or veiled because of the education and there is nothing more important in all the universe than to turn it back on. That is the meaning of life.

One has their right brain veiled as a child and one spends their life trying to unveil it. It does not have to be a lifelong ambition. It can be turned back on in one second and then ones goal in life is to assist others to turn their back on and that is perhaps impossible so one has job security. That is the only purpose in life. Everything else is secondary foolishness.

As a species we played around with fire, written language, and got burned, and now we have to try and undo that mistake. As a species we have to learn how to handle fire without letting it burn us all alive. But first one has to break the curse the invention has caused. One has to focus on the log of fear in their eye first. Whatever you think is more important than that you are wrong, dead wrong. That is the complexity of the two great truths. If one does not understand them they are dead in the water on every level one can be dead in the water. I am not suggesting maybe dead in the water or perhaps dead in the water I am explaining absolutely dead in the water.

It does not matter who your cult leaders think they are. If they do not know the two greatest truths in the universe relative to mankind they are nothing but a fool. They are a fool because their understanding house is built upon soft sand if they do not understand the two greatest truths relative to mankind in all the universe.

One can try to explain away the two great truths but the two great truths are immune to the babblings of fools. A fool cannot grasp truth that is why truth is the domain of the wise. One can try to calculate what the great truths are but the great truths are only detectable by the wise. One can only detect the great truths using intuition and intuition is the strength of right brain and if they have right brain veiled they do not have enough intuition to detect the great truths. This is what the wise teachers in history tried to do. They tried to assist students to understand the great truths. This relates to a great impossibility.

One has to break the curse and thus unveil right brain so they have strong intuition to be able to understand the two great truths yet one cannot break the curse unless they understand the two great truths.

This is impossibility and an indication of how strong the curse is. Simply put, one has to see in order to see they are blind. So these wise beings were able to make the blind see. I am zero for six billion but I am pleased with the job security. I am a master at getting my teeth kicked in but I fall short of being able to make the blind see. I cannot make the blind see so I cannot show them where the sea is. They are all stuck on the shore in the sand so I can't bring them out to sea. I can only tell them the two great truths but they perhaps always see them as lies. I cannot do this impossible thing, the curse is too strong.

Everyone gets killed trying to stop the curse and the curse doesn't ever stop. The sane kill everyone who tries to speak about the curse. The sane kill the ones who try to speak about the curse and then the sane claim they are righteous for doing so, when in reality they hang their self and doom their self to the curse. The sane have been hanging their self for over 5000 years and are totally oblivious to it because they are blind to the two great truths.

No one likes their reality shattered and that is what the two great truths do. The cursed become uneasy when the two great truths are spoken because the two great truths burn them and burn down their house of understandings. The sane can go on and on about what they think truth is but their truth's collapse in the presence of the two great truths. There are only two great truths relative to mankind and if one does not understand them there is no mankind only beasts.- 12:26:26 PM

10/20/2009 3:35:13 AM – Left brain is relative to intellect. Right brain is relative to intuition.
The complexity of the ancient texts is one needs intuition to understand them not intellect. Some of the sane understand these ancient texts are code. Intellect relates to proving everything based on texts or comments from others.

Intuition denotes reading one sentence out of the ancient and understanding what it means without the need to read the previous sentence or the next sentence.
Intuition is understanding or heightened awareness and intellect is knowing or relying on the words of others to make a point. This comment is a good example.
[Amos 5:21 I hate, I despise your feast days, and I will not smell in your solemn assemblies.]

The sane will look at this comment and try to relate it to other comments and try to associate dates or the words so that is makes sense to them. Intuition tells a person exactly what this sentence means without having to look at any other sentence in any other books or the meaning is understood instantly and that is relative to heightened awareness or getting the spirit of the text.

The first words "I hate", hate is not possible in the neutral state of mind, the right brain processes to fast to hold a grudge, but this is a comment that is relative to trying to explain a cerebral feeling and putting it down in words but the words fail at explaining it properly.

It is more proper to say he is displeased with the feasts and assemblies because he is aware of the fruit they represent. A feast and assembly is what the sane call a holiday. A holiday is simply a money making opportunity and the fact they have these holidays in the name of these wise beings is an insult to the wise beings on a level that cannot even be explained.

Perhaps the sane are cerebrating the fact they never understood what any of these wise beings were even saying. Perhaps the sane are celebrating the fact they sacrifice their own first born to demotic. Perhaps the sane are celebrating they were able to butcher most of these wise beings in such short order. Perhaps the sane are celebrating their ability to spit in the face of these wise beings by holding money making opportunities in the name of the wise beings. That's the fruits of the sane, they kill these wise beings and then they make a holiday and tell everyone how much they loved them.

The sane are in a world of anti truth and the deeds they do are symptoms of that. For example Easter is simply a feast for the sane to celebrate the reality they slaughtered a wise being and thus hung their self because it ensured the curse will continue and it has and it does continue. All the holidays relative to these wise beings all across the board are simply feasts to commemorate the sane killing the truth. That is what this means.

[Amos 5:21 I hate, I despise your feast days, and I will not smell in your solemn assemblies.]

I do not hate the sane but I submit their level of darkness is beyond my ability to explain in infinite books.

[Galatians 4:10 Ye observe days, and months, and times, and years.]= the sane.

" I despise your feast days "and "I will not smell in your solemn assemblies."=["your]= the sane = [Galatians 4:10 Ye observe days, and months, and times, and years.]= holiday = sense of time= calendar= calendar is sequenced numbers.- 4:01:17 AM

[Amos 5:10 They hate him that rebuketh in the gate, and they abhor him that speaketh uprightly.] = Gate = the exit out of the mental place one is at when they get the curse

Speaketh uprightly = one who can explain how to break the curse = exit the gate= get out of the mental place on is at once they get the curse = the key holder.

[Galatians 4:10 Ye observe days, and months, and times, and years.] kill the key holder so they remain in the place of suffering/gnashing of teeth because the key holder is the only way for them to get out.

The sane kill the one who can open the gate and free them and this cycle has been going on for over 5000 years because the sane know not what they do. The sane embrace what keeps them locked in the suffering place and kill what can release them from the suffering place. This is the great cycle mankind is trapped in because of this demotic curse. This cycle can be broken on an individual level but perhaps never on a species wide level because the most powerful sane, task masters, will never allow the slaves, in the place of suffering, to be freed.

Moses tried to free the ones who were in the place of suffering. He was a key holder. But the complexity is, it eventually all collapses because the sane cannot grasp what the two greatest truths are. If the two greatest truths are not understood the species goes back to the place of suffering again. So every day the sane throw the tree of knowledge at the children and do not administer it properly and so we hang our self everyday and that is what Judas does. Judas turned in the key holder and in turn he hung the species or the species in killing Jesus hung their self because they doomed their self to the place of suffering. Judas is civilization. Judas is the sane. Judas = [Galatians 4:10 Ye observe days, and months, and times, and years.] = [Amos 5:10 [They](the sane) hate him(the key holder) that rebuketh in the gate, and [they](the sane) abhor him(the key holder) that speaketh uprightly.] - 4:27:16 AM

[Amos 5:21 I hate, I despise your [feast days], and I will not smell in your solemn assemblies.]
Feast days = holiday set at a certain calendar day = calendar requires math and numbers to keep track of = [Galatians 4:10 Ye observe days, and months, and times, and years.] = calendar = sense of time. Math = calendar = left brain sequential conditioning =/ results in, sense of time. Relative to, before the big bang there was no time. Big bang = creation. Creation = time = math and written language = left brain sequential conditioning = one starts to have a sense of time = fall from grace = unsound mind, relative to great fear in the mind =

119

[2 Timothy 1:7 For God hath not given us the spirit of fear; but of power, and of love, and of a sound mind.]

[[Genesis 4:6 And the LORD said unto Cain, Why art thou wroth? and why is thy countenance fallen?] = countenance fallen = unsound mind = left brain sequential conditioning = one has great fear in the mind = math and written language = wroth/wrath/anger = emotions.

"Why art thou wroth?" = Why art thou emotional? = [Luke 9:60 Jesus said unto him, [Let the dead bury their dead]: but go thou and preach the kingdom of God.]

[Let the dead bury their dead] = emotional = covet the dead = emotional over the dead = idolatry = suffering

[Let the dead bury their dead] = "Why art thou wroth?" = Why art thou emotional? = [Genesis 4:5 But unto Cain and to his offering he had not respect. And Cain was very wroth, and his countenance fell.] = One has not applied the remedy to the curse = Abraham and Isaac method =

[[Luke 17:33 ;and whosoever shall lose his life shall preserve it.]

X = state of mind after the education: extreme left brain state of mind = Ego

Y = State of mind after one applies the remedy = No Ego= sound mind left and right brain working equally

So, and whosoever shall lose his life(X) shall preserve it(Y).] = [Submit] to perceived fear of death to silence fear = Socrates said no true philosopher fears death = Jesus defeated death as in his fear of death. = Remedy to curse.]

[Luke 9:60 Jesus said unto him, Let [the dead] bury their dead: but go thou and preach the kingdom of God.] relative to [Acts 10:42 And he commanded us to preach unto the people, and to testify that it is he which was ordained of God to be the Judge of quick [and dead.]]

[the dead] = emotional = [Galatians 4:10 Ye observe days, and months, and times, and years.] = emotional and have a sense of time = cursed , relative to [Genesis 3:14 … the serpent,… thou art cursed above all cattle, and above every [beast] of the field;…]

120

[beast] = [the dead] = emotional = [Galatians 4:10 Ye observe days, and months, and times, and years.] = emotional and have a sense of time = cursed, relative to [Revelation 20:10 And the devil that deceived them was cast into the lake of [fire and brimstone], where [the beast and the false prophet] are, and shall be [tormented day and night for ever and ever.]= suffer] - 5:39:36 AM

["Yes, America is gigantic, but a gigantic mistake."
Sigmund Freud

'That to secure these rights, Governments are instituted among Men, deriving their just powers from the consent of the governed, — That whenever any Form of Government becomes destructive of these ends, it is the Right of the People to alter or to abolish it, and to institute new Government, laying its foundation on such principles and organizing its powers in such form, as to them shall seem most likely to effect their Safety and Happiness. Prudence, indeed, will dictate that Governments long established should not be changed for light and transient causes; and accordingly all experience hath shewn that mankind are more disposed to suffer, while evils are sufferable than to right themselves by abolishing the forms to which they are accustomed.'
Declaration of Independence

"Congress shall make no law respecting an establishment of religion, or prohibiting the free exercise thereof; or abridging the freedom of speech, or of the press; or the right of the people peaceably to assemble, and to petition the Government for a redress of grievances."
First Amendment – Bill of Rights]

There is a spirit in these words. If one is in extreme left brain they can't get the spirit or sense the spirit. The reason America is a gigantic mistake is because it is based on rules to avoid tyranny but the entire world is prone to tyranny. The reason the world is prone to tyranny is because the education conditions one to extreme left brain and in turn makes them very afraid because the hypothalamus and the amygdala stops working properly and so they make a person very afraid and thus prone to fear tactics and in a condition of fear a tyrant thrives, also left brain loves rules right brain does not. Rules get in the way of right brains pattern detection ability.

This is the first spirit of these words [That whenever any Form of Government becomes destructive of these ends, it is the Right of the People to alter or to abolish it, and to institute new Government,] That is a gigantic mistake to add those words to the Declaration of Independence. Those words cannot be understood by someone who is afraid they can only be understood by someone who is fearless. I will tell you something about the people who founded this nation because you are not capable of understanding who they were and you assume they were like you and that is also a gigantic mistake. The reason the founding fathers went to war against the British was because of this [That whenever any Form of Government becomes destructive of these ends, it is the Right of the People to alter or to abolish it,]

[destructive of these ends] = [Congress shall make no law; abridging the freedom of speech,]
The British are not too high on freedom of speech and that is why they are tyrants and that is why the founding fathers watered the tree of liberty with them. You think freedom is signing away freedom of speech. That is all you will ever understand about freedom. You think freedom is rules. [Congress (voters) shall make no law; abridging the freedom of speech,]
It does not matter if 300 million people vote to abridge freedom of speech, which they have, they do not have that freedom or right. The only thing that is going to happen when people abridge freedom of speech is revolution.

I am doing this [That whenever any Form of Government becomes destructive of these ends, it is the Right of the People to alter or to abolish it,] I am suggesting the Government should be abolished because they have abridged the freedom of speech and that means it is [the Right of the People to alter or to abolish it] and that means if the Government resists they deny my rights [it is the Right of the People to alter or to abolish it], and then they get abolished for that also. So it is a double abolishment. The government gets abolished for abridging freedom of speech and then if they resist they get abolished again until there is no government. Now you understand why Freud said this:

"Yes, America is gigantic, but a gigantic mistake."
Sigmund Freud

I get the impression Freud is infinitely wiser than you will ever be. On with the show.

My infinite wrath potential brought home a cold from work and I caught it. I will try to explain what it is like to have a cold in this neutral state of mind so I will start off with saying it is painless. There are no aches and pains. I have a stuffed up nose and I can tell my throat is sore but not because it is sore but because it feels like I remember a sore throat felt like before the accident but it is not sore. So I have a cold and I should feel aches and pains and feel tired and be weak but I am not at all. I am aware I have a cold but I feel no physiological aches that one with a sense of time feels from a cold. I am aware I have a cold but I am not sore or weak from the cold. And that is what this comment is relative to.

[Genesis 3:16 Unto the woman he said, [I will greatly multiply thy sorrow] and thy conception; in sorrow thou shalt bring forth children; and thy desire shall be to thy husband, and he shall rule over thee.]

[I will greatly multiply thy sorrow] = You are doing a lot of suffering you should not be doing. You are suffering in vain. You do not have to be suffering with all the aches and pains but you are and you choose to. This left brain state of mind that education has conditioned you into has turned up all your pain thresholds, mentally, emotionally and physiologically. I am trying to convince you to let go of your suffering and you hate me for that and that is what this comment relates to.

[Neurotics complain of their illness, but they make the most of it, and when it comes to talking it away from them they will defend it like a lioness her young.]
Sigmund Freud

You are neurotic and you love your suffering so suffering is what you have been conditioned to love. You have become suffering = [I will greatly multiply thy sorrow]. You tell me to my face "You have to have fear or you will die." You love your suffering and you assume I am stupid to suggest fear is a delusion of an unsound mind because [they will defend it(illness) like a lioness her young.]

There is a pattern that you would never detect because your right brain is veiled and right brain detects patterns. I will teach you as my little cult followers because all you can do is follow because you can't think for yourself.

"What progress we are making. In the Middle Ages [they] would have burned me. Now [they] are content with burning my books."
Sigmund Freud
"Neurotics complain of their illness, but [they] make the most of it, and when it comes to talking it away from them [they] will defend it like a lioness her young."
Sigmund Freud

[They] = [beast] = [the (mentally slothful, left brain extreme) dead] = emotional = [Galatians 4:10 Ye observe days, and months, and times, and years.] = emotional and have a sense of time = cursed = [I will greatly multiply thy sorrow(emotional and physiological pain)]= [Genesis 3:14 And the LORD God said unto [the serpent], Because thou hast done this, thou art [[cursed] above all cattle], and above every beast of the field; upon thy belly shalt thou go, and dust shalt thou eat all the days of thy life:]

I am only harsh in my words from the point of view of a neurotic who believes words. Someone told me when I was young that I was a failure and not intelligent because I could not spell the word cat properly and I understand that was [they]. That certainly blew it. - 4:24:02 PM

9:01:13 PM – The main symptoms of the curse is a strong sense of time and fear. If you have these symptoms you are cursed and your disbelief does not matter at all. Your enemy is you and that is because you, as in your state of mind, is false.

What you think is good is bad and what you think is bad is good. So you are your own worst enemy. You can try to come up with things you have done that are good and they are all bad. You are simply in hallucination world to such an extreme you sense time. If you said you see little green men walking around you but you don't sense time I would understand you are not hallucinating as bad as I understand you are hallucinating.

Do you know any human being in the history of mankind that writes books and tells people if they sense time they are hallucinating? You are in a position where either I am the most crazy human being in the history of mankind or you are. I can tell you I had an accident and lost my fear of death and woke up or broke the curse accidentally but you cannot understand that or understand what that means because when you try to think your thoughts are your worst enemy. You want to go verify what I say in a book because you have no intuition so you need someone to tell you what you should think because you cannot think on your own. You are already considered lost. You will not understand what I say so I write for ones who come after you so they can understand.

[Matthew 23:33 Ye serpents, ye generation of vipers, how can ye escape the damnation of hell?]

How are you going to escape this mental hallucination world you are in if when you try to figure out how to escape, you always come up with ways not to escape the hallucination world? The reality is your mind is false because its telling you there is time. Your mind is registering time and so your mind is unsound because a sound mind should not be registering time. You are going to assume that is a lie because you didn't read that anywhere in a book. They didn't teach you that in school so it certainly must not be truth because certainly school is about teaching you knowledge not ruining your mind.

This is why I don't talk to you because your mind is in a state called "damnation of hell". You can call it whatever you want but it's not going to break the curse. Whatever you are praying too when you are in this state of mind, "damnation of hell", is of hell. I am not going to get into details with you. You cannot even understand simple truth let alone complex details. I am not suggesting you put yourself into this curse. That is not truth. You were a child and the ones who were suppose to look out for you, sold you for a few silver pieces to the serpent. That is truth. There is no point in getting upset about that because that will not break the curse. Once you break the curse everything will make sense but your mind is in "damnation of hell" and it does not want you to break the curse so it will deceive you and talk you out of breaking the curse.

I understood I was in such fast mental progression shortly after the accident that soon I would be beyond your ability to even understand at all. Am I beyond your ability to even understand at all? I am going one way and you are going the other way and we just keep getting further and further apart. I am mindful I cannot really reach you so I write to myself. - 9:24:17 PM

10/21/2009 9:03:52 AM –

I waited on the bridge surrounded by dark
The clocks were singing, the wind was stark
The greater light was hidden from view
The ones in the cities seldom knew

The greater sight reflected light
When the water below caught it right
The chalice would then overflow
Then sunk into the depths below

The distance was just faded hue
In time that only calendar knew
The heat that came from furnace glow
The greater light cities would not sow

Between the dark convincing light
The shadows of the blinded sight
The current swift that rocks would flow
Confused awareness the depths would know

The current from the shallow pools
Understand the depths for fools
The shallow cannot reach the sea
To swim alone and swim so free

The shallows rush to go nowhere

Their nervousness their only care
I ponder if they understand
They never made it off the sand.

How many times should I suggest
How many times will they detest
The shallows are a prideful band
Their tears are what make up the sand.

How many times could I suggest
How many times could they detest
I do not see the shallows best
I cannot fight their ebbing nest

Should time for me only pause
Yet embrace the shallows with its claws
I cannot find a way to claim
The sand they love is hottest flame

The ease at which their vipers tongue
Drowns out the light with songs unsung
The shallows tension they cannot bare
The stone around their neck and hair

The weight I had I no longer see
The weight has fallen from this tree
The sorrow of the shallows flee
Should time only pause for me

I crossed the river to the sea
The shallows hate that I can see
Their trapped in the shallow pools
Where lovers die and turn to fools

Why do they wait and suffer still
I cannot steer them to the door
They mock and spit at the wall they see
Their calendar keeps them on the shore

Their crescent moon will not allow
Their time so strong their sorrow hark
I cannot steer them from that dark
I only see the shallows mark.

They believe they're on the sea
The sand will never set them free
I must watch their sickened tree
Should time only pause, pause for me? - 10:07:13 AM

The Shallows - http://www.youtube.com/watch?v=ayC_2t8GyU0

11:10:08 AM –
   The emotions and sense of time and the fear, the embarrassment, the rules are all simply baggage and they create a mind that is not focused. The mind has all this clutter caused by all of these things that one perceives are normal. Once the remedy is applied and the right brain is unveiled it turns off all of these clutter aspects and that allows the extreme concentration or what is known as heightened awareness. One cannot concentrate with sense of time and thoughts of past and future and thoughts of embarrassment and lust, and love, and greed, and envy, because these things are not what they appear to be, they are simply clutter that hinders the powerhouse of the mind which is right brain. This left brain education creates mental clutter and one has to apply the remedy to eliminate the clutter or they are doomed to a confused mind and a confused mind creates suffering. - 11:15:38 AM

12:48:11 PM - One truth is what causes the curse and one truth is the remedy to the curse. If one misses what causes the curse they will miss what remedies the curse.

[Job 1:6 Now there was a day when the sons of God came to present themselves before the LORD, [and Satan came also among them.]
Job 1:7 And the LORD said unto Satan, Whence comest thou? Then Satan answered the LORD, and said, [From going to and fro in [the earth], and from walking up and down in it.] = [Galatians 4:10 Ye observe days, and months, and times, and years.]

Job 1:8 And the LORD said unto Satan, Hast thou considered [my servant] Job, that there is [none like him in the earth], [a perfect] and an upright[man], one that feareth God, and [escheweth evil?]= [Revelation 2:10 Fear none of those things which thou shalt suffer: behold, the devil shall cast some of you into prison, that ye may be tried; and ye shall have tribulation ten days: [be thou faithful unto death], and [I will give thee a crown of life.]

[be thou faithful unto death] = [[Luke 17:33 ;and whosoever [shall lose= (face perceived death) his life shall preserve it.]
X = state of mind after the education: extreme left brain state of mind = Ego
Y = State of mind after one applies the remedy = No Ego= sound mind left and right brain working equally
So, and whosoever shall lose his life(X) shall preserve it(Y).] = [Submit] to perceived fear of death to silence fear = Socrates said no true philosopher fears death = Jesus defeated death as in his fear of death. = Remedy to curse.]

[I will give thee a crown of life.] = [Genesis 15:1 … [Fear not], Abram: [I am thy shield, and [thy exceeding great reward.].

[Fear not] + [be thou faithful unto death] + Lose fear of death = [I will give thee a crown of life.]/ [thy exceeding great reward.](unnamable) = unveil right brain/ break curse caused by tree of knowledge.

This accident is a test to see if I can overcome my fear of telling you the truth when you hate the truth. This accident has nothing to do with you breaking the curse it has to do with me breaking the curse. I am trying to break the curse and you just so happen to be a witness to it. I cannot focus on the log of fear in your eye because I must focus on the log of fear in my eye.
You are not even past this point [Genesis 3:6 …..saw that [the tree was good for food], and that it was [pleasant to the eyes], and a tree to be [desired to make one wise], …]
Perhaps you do not know where you are at. Perhaps you know not what you do, what you say, or what you are. I am writing infinite books into infinity, perhaps that bothers you. That perhaps would be

unfortunate if that bothered you, because one might suggest infinity goes on forever and ever. Infinity does not bother me, does it bother you?

[1 John 4:18 [There is no fear] in love; but perfect love casteth out fear: because [fear hath torment.] [[He that feareth] is not made perfect in love.]] = [2 Timothy 1:7 For God [hath not given us the spirit of fear]; but of power, and of love, and of a sound mind.] relative to [Revelation 1:17 And when I saw him, I fell at his feet as dead. And he laid his right hand upon me, saying unto me, [Fear not]; [[I am] the [first and the last:]]

[He that feareth] = [spirit of fear]= [Galatians 4:10 Ye observe days, and months, and times, and years.] = unsound mind
[I am] = no sense of time or in the now
[first and the last:] = Random access = right brain

[hath not given us the spirit of fear]+ [Fear not] = Sound mind

7:01:24 PM – Everything I suggest comes down to one question. Is it in the realm of possibility that 12 years of left brain education, written language and math, could alter the mind into an unsound state?

Do you think a teacher or an education board can ever answer that question? Do you think anyone you know understands the mind and the brain? Do you know anyone who has no sense of time? Your chances of answering the question that maybe man invented something that has unintended consequences are zero.

You cannot believe mankind invented something that has such far reaching detrimental effects on the mind of children because a child's mind is not even fully developed when they get the education. You can only get wiser from the point you are at now. You speak of the importance of responsibility. Mentally raping children is not responsible. I am not concerned about you or your hallucinations because I have written you off. You are not a concern to me. I am not my brother's keeper. I am concerned you are going to do to children what you did to me. That means we have a battle on our hands to the death doesn't it? I understand you want a battle to the death.

I understand you think you can win this battle to the death. I am pleased with a battle to the death. I am humbled you wish to fight a battle to the death against me. I do not mind repeat performances. I want you to forget everything I have ever written and that way when I blindside you it will not hurt as much. Deny your emotions grasshopper. - 7:13:30 PM

10/22/2009 8:12:58 AM – One may defend their honor but it will cost them their grace and without grace one has no honor.

3:17:54 PM – Never confuse words with physical violence. When one starts to assume a sentence is the same as physical violence they are hallucinating to the point they are dangerous.
A word is a sound and a written word is a sound and both are created by thoughts. If one cannot vent their thoughts and thus words on all levels then there is time for a physical revolution so that becomes possible. Some of the sane understand words are the same a physical violence so their main goal is to stop thoughts which is what words are so they are dangerous. Because our species is in this left brain extreme state of mind and thus unviable mentally as a species nature itself is looking to make us destroy ourselves because we are so far out of harmony. The sane can be defeated with words because they cannot think properly so they can be manipulated like illusions and bend to ones will. The most important thing is once you apply the remedy you focus on your objectives and avoid getting into arguments with the sane because their main goal is to make you destroy yourself because they are cursed and can only begets the curse and are destruction unto their self. The main goal after one applies the remedy is to work on ways to talk the sane out of their suicide plunge. The sane are your friends but they are under the influence of something that is not easily explainable in words.

[Exodus 32:19 And it came to pass, as soon as he came nigh unto the camp, that he saw the calf, and the dancing: and Moses' anger waxed hot, and he cast the tables out of his hands, and brake them beneath the mount.]
The sane have a delusional impression these wise beings were popular. The sane are under the delusional impression these wise

beings were running around and everyone liked them. The sane hated these wise beings and the sane still hate these wise beings and the sane will hate these wise beings into infinity.

Moses risked his life after he broke the curse by going back to free people from the taskmaster and then he tried to explain how they could break the curse and they spit in his face. The sane spit in his face now and tomorrow and into infinity. That is the fruits of the sane. The fruits of the sane are rotten because the tree of the sane are rotten, their mind, and so the tree must be ripped out of the ground and a new tree must be planted. That is what this means [Luke 17:33 ;and whosoever shall lose his life shall preserve it.]

One has to kill their self mentally because after one gets the education their self is mental death. Your cult leader is not going to tell you that is truth because your cult leader is only in it for the money. If you cult leader understood the remedy and told you it, then there would be no reason for you to keep giving him money. A cult leader just keeps you hanging on and keeps asking for money but never tells you the final remedy and that's how you know they are a cult leader.

The reality is your cult leader does not know the remedy because if they did they wouldn't be charging for it. Your cult leader is this: [Matthew 7:21 Not every one that saith unto me, Lord, Lord, shall enter into the kingdom of heaven; but he that doeth [the will] of my Father which is in heaven.]

The will is the remedy, the remedy is the Abraham and Isaac method or the [Luke 17:33 ;and whosoever shall lose his life shall preserve it.] or submit to perceived fear of death. I prefer to just say: Go sit in a cemetery at night until you have brain function. Do not leave that dark cemetery until you have brain function. You do not have brain function because you perceive time. So you need to sit in that cemetery until you do not perceive time at all. That big scary ghost in your hallucinated mind surely will kill you before you have no sense of time and that is when you submit and allow it to kill you.

[Matthew 7:21 Not every one that saith unto me, Lord, Lord, shall enter into the [kingdom of heaven;] = [kingdom of heaven;] = no sense of time

unsound mind = [spirit of fear] = [2 Timothy 1:7 For God hath not given us the spirit of fear; but of power, and of love, and of a sound mind.]

These mental symptoms, sense of time and fear, are relative to ones fruits or deeds, for example sense of time means rush or impatience, no sense of time means relaxed and patient, both patience and impatience are fruits and both are relative to the observer. Relative to a nervous wreck that senses time waiting in line five minutes is being patient. Relative to a being with no sense of time, waiting 5000 years is patience.

Just because one can say the word Lord or God does not mean you break the curse. You underestimate the curse if you perceive you can break it by saying the word Lord or God. You wish in your wildest delusions you could just break the curse by saying a few choice words. If your cult leader says you can, they are a liar and anti-truth.

Why don't you go ask your school if they have any right brain, random access, fear conditioning classes in their curriculum equal to the left brain sequential education. Better yet ask them if they have a sense of time. You think everything is just fine because you see darkness as light.

Your eyes are your enemy. I am an accident so I am compelled to suggest ways you can wake up to reality but I am already fully aware none of these wise beings could convince you to wake up so how on earth am I going to convince you. How can I convince you if none of these wise beings could convince you?

That is an indication of how powerful the curse is. You do not even believe the curse is caused by the tree of knowledge, written language and math, so you cannot believe the second great truth which is the remedy which is : [Luke 17:33 ;and whosoever shall lose his life shall preserve it.], so you do not really stand a chance so I find no reason to try.

I do not edit my books to make them look pleasing to you because you cannot understand them anyway. I am not going to try to reason with you because you cannot be reasoned with. Reasoning with rabidity requires imagination and creativity. If you could buy your way out of the curse with a little bit of money or a few choice words you would have by now, grasshopper.- 3:55:33 PM

5:08:53 PM – Intelligence tests based on written language and math are simply tests to demonstrate how well a being can follow rules and think sequentially and both of these aspects are left brain.

So a being that does well at these "intelligence tests" is a good sheep, follower of rules, and has lots of sequential thoughts so very little complexity in thoughts, right brain. Any person who says "One needs this education to survive in today's world." is really saying "You have to hate right brain to survive in today's world."

One cannot think out of the box or adapt or be creative when they have been conditioned into extreme left brain so they are simply not even viable as a thinking being because those attributes are right brain. Once a person graduates high school they have proven to the world they are a good sheep and can follow all the rules without questioning them and they have no creativity or complexity in thoughts and they are afraid of a bad haircut, and the greatest thoughts they will ever have are sequential thoughts.

That is what you get a graduation certificate for, so you can let the world know you are mentally unviable as a being. You got suckered in and manipulated and fear tactics were used on you so you would veil your complex right brain and that certificate only proves you are a Grade A Sucker.

You are going to have to think for yourself one day and you cannot do that because you are mentally hallucinating so much you perceive time. Any creature that cannot think for itself is doomed. What are you going to do when there is no safety net and all these beings your trusted and count on to think for you are nowhere to be found?

Society has conditioned you with their wisdom education to follow rules and think sequentially so you are doomed, you are a write off. In a situation that requires one to think for their self with no safety net you are valueless. You have no worth in a situation that requires complex thoughts and complex adaptation. That is why you are in a cage because you cannot be trusted to think, or make decisions. That is what the taskmaster wants. He wants slaves that cannot think or make decisions so they will always rely on the task master to tell them what to do.

You pay people to tell you what you should do because you cannot think with any complexity to answer your own questions. Why can't you answer your own questions? Because you have been conditioned to rely on others to tell you what to think.

You can breathe and take a piss on your own but that is as far as it goes. You need someone to tell you how to eat, how to speak, how to write, how to function. Why are you such a sucker? You believe the stupidest things are truth. You believe if you cannot master a sequential based manmade invention it means you are not intelligent even though this invention only came on the scene 5000 years ago. We as a species have lived for over 200,000 years and all the sudden some idiot invents language and because you cannot master it flawlessly they tell you that you are not intelligent, and you are dumb enough to believe it.

In a world where they tell children you cannot live without money it is best to avoid living. Is all the money you have now because you got the education and are mentally so unviable you sense time, worth it? Is the money worth you not having a viable mind? Will the money you have stop you from hallucinating? Maybe some more drugs will help you to escape hallucination world you have been thrown into by the society you trust so much.

You have to go get some therapy because you love the ones who mentally raped you and you are not intelligent enough to understand that. I don't speak to people who are hallucinating and then deny they are hallucinating. Are you smart enough to understand there are no laws against brainwashing people or mentally abusing people? Do you ever question why there are no laws against mentally abusing people?

You have been brainwashed to the point you sense time and you fear words. One cannot be mentally abused worse than that but there are no laws against doing that to a person. What location do you

135

think allows people to mentally abuse other people to the point the people abused are left hallucinating and suffering for the rest of their life? Are you still trying to figure out what the tree of knowledge is? I deny that you are that stupid. You cannot possibly be that stupid that you still do not understand what the tree of knowledge is. There is nothing in the universe that stupid except demons. That certainly blew it.- 5:40:59 PM

10/23/2009 9:42:19 AM

It does not bother me so much, that you would say I'm lying
I cannot convince you either way, that's why I won't be trying.
The task is just too harsh to face, I cannot lift the plough.
Indifference is my only friend, as cold as you are now.
- 9:56:49 AM

10:12:59 AM –
Should I escape on beams of light,
The darker ones sad to trained sight,
They are not lost as much as blind,
They are not evil just not refined.
I should not question where they come
They know what they must do
They cannot see the beams of light, only beams of blue.
-10:18:02 AM

10:19:15 AM –
They cannot soar above the sea
The wings they've clipped enough for me
They will not smote so suffer still
The damaged wings and blinded ill
I cannot heal to see their rot
Their garments desire, they cast the lot.
     -    10:26:46 AM

10:27:11 AM –
It never was that I was weak
The words that would not reach the peak

It never was that I was poor
The words could not steer to the door
It never was that I could fail
The words were not sufficient grail
It never was impatience wait
The word would always veil the gate
It never was my greatest loss
The words that covered majestic trees with moss
- 10:32:33 AM

4:14:30 PM – There is no way to prove that many years of written language, reading and math conditions the mind into extreme left brain or veils the mind. Once in a while in history beings break this veiled mind state and accomplish some very profound things and that is the proof.

The deeds of the beings that break the veiled state of mind are the proof but the sane can never understand that. These wise beings from thousands of years ago wrote texts that are still being read and republished today and that is the proof.

This is why one story suggests having faith the size of a mustard seed because there will never be a way to prove what this tree of knowledge does to the human mind. The damage is on a mental level not a physiological level. My MRI checked out normal. My EEG checked out normal. The sane are still looking at Einstein's brain trying to figure out why he was so special. The sane are always looking for proof when there is no proof, only fruits. There are only fruits of a good tree, mind. The sane are never going to find a good tree they are only going to see fruits of a good tree. You are going to keep mentally raping children because I cannot prove that is in fact what you are doing, mentally raping children. You have the numbers so might makes right.

The only thing that is right in this world is the world is full of mentally unviable morons who are hallucinating to the point they sense time. This world is going to keep mentally raping children because I cannot prove it to them. None of the wise beings could prove it to them either. The sane killed Socrates for corrupting the minds of the youth. They killed Jesus for saying suffer the children too many times.

The sane = [They] = [beast] = [the dead] = emotional = [Galatians 4:10 Ye observe days, and months, and times, and years.] = emotional and have a sense of time = mentally cursed = [I will greatly multiply thy sorrow]= [Genesis 3:14 And the LORD God said unto [the serpent], Because thou hast done this(got the education), thou art [[cursed] above all cattle], and above every beast of the field; upon thy belly shalt thou go, and dust shalt thou eat all the days of thy life:]= [the serpent].
[Revelation 13:18 Here is wisdom. Let him that hath understanding count the number of the beast: for it is the number of a [man]; and his number is Six hundred threescore and six.]
[Man]= [Genesis 11:5 And the LORD came down to see the city and the [tower](cities), which the children of [men] builded.]= [and his number is Six hundred threescore and six.]= [Judges 8:17 And he beat down the [tower] of Penuel, and [slew the men of the city.]]

[Judges 1:17 And Judah went with Simeon his brother, and they [slew the Canaanites(men)] that inhabited Zephath, and (utterly destroyed it). And the name of the city was called Hormah.] = [Judges 9:49 And [all the people(men)] likewise cut down every man his bough, and followed Abimelech, and put them to the hold, and [set the hold on fire upon them]; so that all the [men of the tower] of Shechem died also, about a thousand men and women.]

[men of the tower] = [Genesis 11:5 And the LORD came down to see the city and the [tower](cities), which the children of [men] builded.] = The sane = [They] = [beast] = [the dead] = emotional = [Galatians 4:10 Ye observe days, and months, and times, and years.] = emotional and have a sense of time = mentally cursed = [I will greatly multiply thy sorrow]= [Genesis 3:14 And the LORD God said unto [the serpent], Because thou hast done this(got the education), thou art [[cursed] above all cattle], and above every beast of the field; upon thy belly shalt thou go, and dust shalt thou eat all the days of thy life:]= [the serpent].

[The sane] = Show me a *sane man* and I will cure him for you. - Carl Jung

[Judges 9:52 And Abimelech came unto the [tower], and [fought against it], and went hard unto the door of the tower to [burn it with fire.]
[Tower] = civilization
Civilization = conditions the children with the education and veils their right brain = 'Children are educated by [what the grown-up is] and not by his talk.' -Carl Jung = cursed beget cursed

[what the grown-up is] = [Genesis 11:5 And the LORD came down to see the city and the [tower](cities/civilization), which the children of [men] builded.] = The sane = [They] = [beast] = [the dead] = emotional = [Galatians 4:10 Ye observe days, and months, and times, and years.] = emotional and have a sense of time = mentally cursed = [I will greatly multiply thy sorrow]= [Genesis 3:14 And the LORD God said unto [the serpent], Because thou hast done this(got the education), thou art [[cursed] above all cattle], and above every beast of the field; upon thy belly shalt thou go, and dust shalt thou eat all the days of thy life:]= [the serpent].

"The healthy man does not torture others - generally it is the tortured who turn into torturers."
Carl Jung = The ones who get the education are conditioned into extreme left brain state of mind and that is torture relative to [I will greatly multiply thy sorrow (condition their own children into the curse/extreme left brain state)]= [Genesis 3:14 And the LORD God said unto [the serpent(and his number is Six hundred threescore and six.)(carbon 12(6 proton, 6 neutrons, 6 electrons) / matter / material focused as opposed to cerebral focused(right brain))]], Because thou hast done this(got the education), thou art [[(mentally)cursed] above all cattle], and above every beast of the field; upon thy belly shalt thou go, and dust shalt thou eat all the days of thy life:]= [the serpent].
After they are conditioned and thus mentally tortured they do the same to their first born and if they do it to their first born they will

also do it to all their children. = [generally it is the tortured who turn into torturers.]

10:29:26 PM – [James 1:8 A [double minded man] is [unstable in all his ways.]] relative to [2 Timothy 1:7 For God hath not given us the [spirit of fear]; but of power, and of love, and of a [sound mind.]] [double minded man] = [spirit of fear] = crescent moon mind, strong left brain, veiled right brain = mentally [unstable in all his ways.] = [Galatians 4:10 Ye observe days, and months, and times, and years.] = emotional and have a sense of time = mentally cursed = [I will greatly multiply thy sorrow]= [Genesis 3:14 And the LORD God said unto [the serpent], Because thou hast done this(got the education), thou art [[cursed] above all cattle], and above every beast of the field; upon thy belly shalt thou go, and dust shalt thou eat all the days of thy life:]= [the serpent].

[sound mind.] = 50/50 right and left brain active, harmony in mind= reverse of [Galatians 4:10 Ye observe days, and months, and times, and years.] = no sense of time.

[Romans 3:16 [Destruction and misery(*)] are in [their] ways:]

[Destruction and misery] = [double minded man] = [spirit of fear] = crescent moon mind, strong left brain veiled right brain = mentally [unstable in all his ways.] = [Galatians 4:10 Ye observe days, and months, and times, and years.] = emotional and have a sense of time = mentally cursed = [I will greatly multiply thy sorrow(*)]= [Genesis 3:14 And the LORD God said unto [the serpent], Because thou hast done this(got the education), thou art [[cursed(*)] above all cattle], and above every beast of the field; upon thy belly shalt thou go, and dust shalt thou eat all the days of thy life:]= [the serpent].

[their] = [men of the tower] = [Genesis 11:5 And the LORD came down to see the city and the [tower](cities), which the children (the men condition their children with the education) of [men] builded.] = The sane = [They] = [beast] = [the dead] = emotional = [Galatians 4:10 Ye observe days, and months, and times, and years.] = emotional and have a sense of time = mentally cursed = [I will greatly multiply

140

thy sorrow]= [Genesis 3:14 And the LORD God said unto [the serpent], Because thou hast done this(got the education), thou art [[cursed] above all cattle], and above every beast of the field; upon thy belly shalt thou go, and dust shalt thou eat all the days of thy life:]= [the serpent].

[Acts 13:10 And said, O full of all [subtilty(*)] and all mischief, thou [child of the devil], thou enemy of all [righteousness], wilt thou not cease to pervert the [right ways] of the Lord?

[subtilty(*)] =[Genesis 3:1 Now the serpent was more [subtil(*)] than any beast of the field which the LORD God had made. And he said unto the woman, Yea, hath God said, Ye shall not eat of every tree of the garden?] = the education is subtle, it slowly conditions the mind to the left and it is difficult to even tell but one slowly starts to show symptoms = = [Galatians 4:10 Ye observe days, and months, and times, and years.(sense of time)] AND [2 Timothy 1:7 For God hath not given us the [[spirit of fear](lots of fear)]; but of power, and of love, and of a sound mind.] = [Genesis 3:10 And he said, I heard thy voice in the garden, and [[I was afraid](post education)],[because I was naked; and I hid myself](embarrassment).= strong emotions / Contrast pre-education [Genesis 2:25 And they were both naked, the man and his wife, and [were not ashamed]]

Post education = [because I was naked; and I hid myself] = fear of nudity, words, the dark etc = [James 1:8 A [double minded man] is [unstable in all his ways.]] = emotional problems

Pre education = [Genesis 2:25 And they were both naked, the man and his wife, and [were not ashamed]] = sound mind = no fear or emotional problems.

[Luke 10:3 Go your ways: behold, I send you forth as [lambs] among [wolves.]]

[lambs] = sound minded = cerebral = not prone to violence
[wolves.] = unsound minded = prone to violence = [double minded man] = [spirit of fear] = crescent moon mind, strong left brain veiled

right brain = mentally [unstable in all his ways.] = [Galatians 4:10 Ye observe days, and months, and times, and years.] = emotional and have a sense of time = mentally cursed = [I will greatly multiply thy sorrow(*)]= [Genesis 3:14 And the LORD God said unto [the serpent], Because thou hast done this(got the education), thou art [[cursed(*)] above all cattle], and above every beast of the field; upon thy belly shalt thou go, and dust shalt thou eat all the days of thy life:]= [the serpent] = [1 John 2:18 Little children(lambs), it is the last time: and as ye have heard that antichrist(wolves) shall come, even now are there many [antichrists(wolves)]; whereby we know that it is the last time.]

\

[antichrists(wolves)] = [1 Corinthians 15:37 And that which thou sowest, thou sowest not that body that shall be, but [bare grain], it may chance of wheat, or of some other grain:
[antichrists(wolves)]=[bare grain] = unsound mentally = bare grain = bad fruits or no fruits

[Luke 13:19 It is like a grain of [mustard seed], which a man took, and cast into his garden; and it grew, and [waxed a great tree; and the fowls of the air lodged in the branches of it.]]

[mustard seed] = right brain is just the other hemisphere of the brain but it is light years more powerful than left brain = [waxed a great tree; and the fowls of the air lodged in the branches of it.]] = one that is cursed must have faith of a mustard seed to understand they are cursed by the tree of knowledge and then apply the fear not remedy and then they will grow a great tree with great fruits = unveil right brain -11:04:10 PM

Fear encourages mental confusion and reduces concentration.
If one is afraid of the world they are afraid of their self.
When one is punished for speaking their mind they are being punished for exercising their mind.
When a word becomes illegal, revolution becomes legal.
Show me your greatest wisdom and I will show you your greatest misunderstanding.
Get your facts straight but first get straight facts.

The sun is not aware he shines so bright.
Everyone should know one person with no sense of time, preferably one's self.

12:31:58 PM – Money has not solved any problem it has not first created.

[Revelation 21:11 Having the [glory of God]: and her light was like unto a stone most precious, even like a jasper stone,[clear as crystal];] relative to [2 Timothy 1:7 For God [hath not given us the spirit of fear]; but of power, and of love, and of a [sound mind.]]]
[clear as crystal] = [sound mind.] = a mind not cluttered with fear which is the reverse of [the spirit of fear] So [glory of God] = [sound mind.] = absence of spirit of fear which is why fear not or the Abraham and Isaac technique, etc is the remedy to the extreme left brain state.

[Revelation 18:21 And a mighty angel took up a stone like a [great millstone], and cast it into the sea, saying, Thus with violence shall that great city Babylon be thrown down, and shall be found no more at all.]
[great millstone] = written language and math /demotic/tree of knowledge, cast it into the sea means they do away with it because it is too dangerous to mess with, city of Babylon is civilization , and it will be destroyed because of the great millstone. Simply put these are nice inventions but they have an unintended side effect and that is they condition the mind to extreme left brain and that's the retarded aspect of the two hemispheres and an unviable species cannot stand, relative to [Genesis 2:17 But of the tree of the knowledge of good and evil, thou shalt not eat of it: for in the day that thou eatest thereof [thou shalt surely die.]]]
So [the spirit of fear] = unsound mind = [thou shalt surely die.] as a species.
These wise beings understood that and that is why they did this :
[Genesis 19:24 Then the LORD rained upon Sodom and upon Gomorrah(civilization) brimstone and fire from the LORD out of heaven;

25 And he [(destroyed)overthrew those cities], and all the plain, and [all the inhabitants of the cities(killed all the beings in the cities who got the education because they were of unsound mind)], and that which grew upon the ground.]

Behind every misunderstanding is an understanding waiting to be misunderstood.-1:41:33 PM

[Acts 15:10 Now therefore why tempt ye God, to put a yoke upon the neck of the disciples, which neither our fathers nor we were able to bear?]

This yoke is the tree of knowledge in relation to convincing people that the written language and math, sequential left brain based, is hindering their mind to a great extreme. "Which neither our fathers nor we were able to bear.' Suggests who difficult it is to convince a person who was taken as a child and conditioned into this extreme left brain state that they are of unsound mind.

They tried to explain the symptoms = to [2 Timothy 1:7 For God [hath not given us the spirit of fear]; but of power, and of love, and of a [sound mind.]]

Fear. You shouldn't have fear to such an extreme. One should have shades of fear not profound fear to the point one thinks a word or music or a picture is going to doom them or harm them, that us a symptom of an unsound mind because the hypothalamus is not working properly. Everything is relative to the observer. If you believe a word or a picture or a sound or music is going to harm you. If your mind is saying a word or picture or song is going to harm you I cannot convince you it will not. If your mind is telling you after you watch a scary movie and turn out the lights you better turn on the lights because a bad thing gets you, I cannot convince you that you are just hallucinating because the hallucination is real to the observer. I use to be afraid of the dark and so I would run and turn on the lights when my mind said I should. I am an accident and my mind no longer tells me to run and turn on the light and I no longer get scared from the dark or words or music. I cannot convince you because ones far wiser than me could not convince you. Ones who got slaughtered while trying to convince you could not convince you.

[Acts 15:10 Now therefore why tempt ye God, to [put a yoke upon the neck of the disciples, which neither our fathers nor we were able to bear?]]
[Mark 15:34 And at the ninth hour Jesus cried with a loud voice, saying, Eloi, Eloi, lama sabachthani? which is, being interpreted, My God, my God, why hast thou forsaken me?]

[put a yoke upon the neck of the disciples, which neither our fathers nor we were able to bear?]= [why hast thou forsaken me?]

'If one does not understand a person, one tends to regard him as a fool.'
Carl Jung

[Revelation 12:12 Therefore rejoice, [ye heavens, and ye that dwell in them.] [Woe to the inhabiters of the earth and of the sea!] for the devil is come down unto you, having great wrath, because he knoweth that he hath but a short time.]

[ye heavens, and ye that dwell in them.] = ones who apply the remedy and achieve the cerebral(heaven) state of mind, sound mind = [lambs] = sound minded = cerebral = not prone to violence = cerebral based/thinkers

[Woe to the inhabiters of the earth and of the sea!] = [wolves.] = unsound minded = prone to violence = [double minded man] = [spirit of fear] = crescent moon mind, strong left brain veiled right brain = mentally [unstable in all his ways.] = [Galatians 4:10 Ye observe days, and months, and times, and years.] = emotional and have a sense of time = mentally cursed = [I will greatly multiply thy sorrow(*)]= [Genesis 3:14 And the LORD God said unto [the serpent], Because thou hast done this(got the education), thou art [[cursed(*)]] above all cattle], and above every beast of the field; upon thy belly shalt thou go, and dust shalt thou eat all the days of thy life:]= [the serpent] = [1 John 2:18 Little children(lambs), it is the last time: and as ye have heard that antichrist(wolves) shall come, even now are there many [antichrists(wolves)]; whereby we

145

know that it is the last time.] = materialistic based/ violent in their ways, [for the devil is come down unto you(you are of the beast)]

[he knoweth that he hath but a short time.] = impatient = senses time = [Galatians 4:10 Ye observe days, and months, and times, and years.]

[Revelation 12:14 And to the woman were given two wings of a great eagle(America), that she might fly into the wilderness(free the people as Moses did when he freed them and brought them back to the wilderness), into her place, where she is nourished for a time, and times, and half a time, from the face of the serpent.]

[Revelation 11:18 And the nations were angry(the sane hate my books), and thy wrath is come, and the time of the dead(the dead have a sense of time), that they should be judged(certainly you are being judged), and that thou shouldest give reward unto thy servants the prophets(I am giving the ones who waited what they waited for) , and to the saints, and them that fear thy name, small and great; and shouldest destroy them(the ones who sense time and destroy the environment and the children's minds) which destroy the earth.]

[Revelation 10:6 And sware by him that liveth for ever and ever, who created heaven, and the things that therein are, [and the earth, and the things that therein are, and the sea,] and the things which are therein, that there should be time no longer:]

[that there should be time no longer:] = it's time to get rid of the ones who sense time because they are going to keep mentally raping the children and they be reasoned with and they are the serpent and of unsound mind = [and shouldest destroy them(the ones who sense time and destroy the environment and the children's minds) which destroy the earth.]

These comments are why Abraham and Lot did and what Moses did. One cannot reason with the sane so they can only be killed because no matter what happens they love their whore demotic and they will ruin more children than anyone can ever convinced others to apply the remedy. Every time one person is convinced to wake up from the curse the sane curse vast amounts of children into the curse by way of the education. The curse can never be broken so Armageddon is the only answer and this is the battle of the minds or the battle of good and evil or the battle of the Samaritan. No one wants to protect the children because they have to fight an army of beasts.

[John 15:14 Ye are my friends, if ye do whatsoever I command you.] this comment is relative to him asking people to fight against the beast that numbers the sand in the sea, the ones with a sense of time who have the curse and the beast has all the weapons and might. This is relative to David and Goliath, the lambs against the pack of wolves.

One who fights a pack of wolves to protect the children = [John 15:13 Greater love hath no man than this, that a man lay down his life for his friends.]

So all the way from Adam to Mohammed these wise beings where trying to save the children from the beasts that kept veiling their mind like a crescent moon with the education, written language and math. They died trying to protect children because they knew if the education kept going the whole species would be of unsound mind and we would be doomed as a species.

It is 1500 years after Mohammed. It is far too late to fix this situation now. The abominations will continue to condition the children with no thought of the cause and effect of twelve years of hardcore sequential left brain,conditioning and the cycle of producing mentally damaged children will continue until our species erupts into a frenzy of war against itself because a house divided, an unsound mind cannot last in a system based on equilibrium or harmony.

[Revelation 2:23 And I will [kill her children with death]; and all the churches shall know that I am he which searcheth the reins and hearts: and I will give unto every one of you according to your works.]

[kill her children with death] = children are educated at an age before their mind can even develop and its all left brain sequential education

(ABC's, 123) and so the children mentally die which means their mind is veiled, all sequential slothful left brain and right brain in turn is essentially turned off = crescent moon mind

[3 John 1:4 I have no greater joy than to [hear that my children walk in truth.]]

[hear that my children walk in truth.] = means a child is educated properly, verbally at least until they are old enough, and perhaps educated by a teacher who knows how to educate a child with the hardcore sequential invention without leaving the child's mind veiled. There is no school in America I know of that does anything but mentally rapes children because they have no idea how to properly use these "tools" without destroying the mind of the child in the process. It is not important if you do not believe that or understand that because you have been judged to nothing more than dust and complicit in the mental raping of children but dust in case you haven't noticed. I do not care much for mental rapists of children.

[1 John 4:4 Ye are of God, little children, and have overcome them: because greater is he that is in you, [than he that is in the world.]]

[than he that is in the world.] relates to the serpent, the one of this world, the tree of knowledge, one needs the knowledge to make it in the world. So John is saying, forget the tree of knowledge the one within you, right brain, is more valuable than this invention the sane suggest you need to be in the world or accepted in the world. Some of these apostles were killed for the same reason Socrates was killed, corrupting the minds of the youth, They were telling children avoid that education because it ruins your mind and your mind is more valuable than that invention called demotic, script and math. The sane killed Socrates 500 years before the apostles for telling the youth the inherit problem with these inventions called written language and math.

The deeper reality is this education may not even be education it may just be a way to turn people into slaves by making them mentally slothful and prone to fear. It's not education its sedation. Of course that's what it is. We as a species were far too smart to control so we had to be sedated to make good slaves. There is nothing this education has given anyone but a slothful mind, lots of fear and lots of suffering. You be a good like cage monkey and act like you didn't just read that.

All these religions are simply beings who woke up from the sedation and tried to tell everyone they were being sedated by a Trojan horse and in turn they were slaughtered by the taskmaster or the taskmasters minions. I would not tell you that if it was not true. I detect these ancient texts are code because they would be killed if they just came out and said what they wanted to say. They were killed anyway but because their texts were in code they survived because few could even understand what the code meant. That way the texts would keep being printed and reproduced so one day when someone woke up they could be translated and explained perhaps in a time when people would not be killed for explaining the texts for what they really mean.

People are sedated as children into a slothful state of mind so they can be controlled easily and they also are prone to fear because this conditioning makes the hypothalamus fear mechanism exaggerated. The book 1984 talks about the thought police. If one takes a child and conditions them into extreme left brain that child will be very slothful mentally and very afraid and easy to control. This means people who kill their self are subconsciously, or right brain, aware something is wrong with this whole situation and they want out. That is why the comment The meek shall inherit the earth was suggested because only the ones who are suicidal are prone to wake up from the sedation and that is because they may come close to death but then not actually die and that triggers the hypothalamus and the amygdala back into working order and the sedation is cancelled.

Mohammed went to a cave when he was 40 because he was distraught with life and he "mediated" and woke up. Buddha left his home and family and "mediated" and starved and woke up. Buddha said I am not the Messiah I am simply awake. Awake denotes one who has cancelled the sedation. Education is the opiate of the masses. That is absolute reality. I am awake but your sure as hell are not. You go ahead and ponder that with that big sequential logic of yours grasshopper. - 9:00:48 PM

11:23:02 PM – [2 Peter 2:14 Having eyes full of adultery, and that cannot cease from sin; beguiling unstable souls: an heart they have exercised with covetous practices; [cursed children]:] relative to [Genesis 3:17 And unto Adam he said, Because thou hast hearkened unto the voice of thy wife, and hast eaten of the tree, of which I commanded thee, saying, Thou shalt not eat of it: [cursed is the ground for thy sake]; in sorrow shalt thou eat of it all the days of thy life;]
Cursed beget cursed. [cursed is the ground for thy sake]; = [cursed children]

What has their education given them? Ways to destroy each other and the environment and the children's minds and their minds. They have nothing to show for all their efforts so they are vanity. I am infinitely interested in finding out if the sane can repay the debt they owe for all the minds they have ruined with their assumptions of wisdom education.

10/25/2009 3:20:10 PM – Genesis translated from the Hebrew word Bereshit which means in the beginning when translated to Greek it means the birth or origin. Hebrew is a part of a Semitic or Arabic group of languages that goes back to 3000 BC. The problem with that is it is assumed Genesis dates back to either 500 BC or 1000 BC. I understand Adam was one of the first to break this "curse" and document it. So that means Genesis in relation to the beginning relates to the beginning of the curse. This is obvious because it relates to the beginning of time. One of the main symptom of the curse is [Galatians 4:10 Ye observe days, and months, and times, and years.] This is relative to the end of time which means the end of the curse and a symptom of the curse is sense of time and it is also in random access so it's backwards.
[Daniel 12:9 And he said, Go thy way, Daniel: for the words are closed up and sealed till the time of the end.]
[till the time of the end.] should be "until the end of time."[for the words are closed up] words is written language and sealed up means stop using the written language and this will bring about the end of time, or this breaks the curse. If one never gets the many years of

sequential education they will not go extreme left brain and they will not show a symptom of the curse, sense of time.

This can be understood better if one looks at Native Americans, they did not have written language and they saw the oneness in everything or everything as a whole and they also lived in harmony with the environment. When the ones who got the curse arrived in America there were 60 million bison and today there are 300,000. That's an indication the ones with the curse cannot live in harmony because they are mentally unsound, have the curse, and thus sense time.

So the first five chapters of Genesis talk about Adam and then it starts off the sixth chapter talking about Noah. This means Adam wrote the first five books up to 5000 years ago and was one of the first to break the curse and explain what it was caused by, the tree of knowledge. His text survived and ever so often someone else would break the curse and add their take on the curse. These ancient texts are simply a historical record of the curse.

It could be looked at as the many people who broke the curse including how they dealt with it and how they figured out how to break the curse. As it progresses the solutions for dealing with the ones cursed increase. Abraham and Lot were at a stage the curse was so far spread they were burning the cities down of the ones cursed and killing them all. I understand the story of Noah is relative to killing everyone who is cursed and just keeping the ones who were not cursed or ones who broke the curse. This did not really happen but it was an idea.

So then after Noah, Abraham started using that idea. Simply put, burn down the cities of men, the cursed, and kill them all. That's the only way to stop the curse because the cursed beget cursed. One is cursed they have a child and they educate that child and curse it. The curse is self perpetuating. In China they have found some script that dates back to 6000 BC. This indicates this script invention started popping up all over the world and slowly people starting breaking the curse it caused. This was not an isolated occurrence. Numbers and math goes back even further perhaps as far as 20,000 years. The problem with counting is eventually you have to sequence the digits, one greater than the other. So the counting was some left brain sequential conditioning but then along came written language, demotic, and it was a double dose of left brain sequential conditioning. Then it was thought these inventions math and written language would make one wise so everyone started doing it.

These inventions do not make one wise, they make one knowledgeable. Knowledge is relative to memorization and wisdom is relative to intuition. Intuition is the realm of right brain. - 4:06:21 PM

[Genesis 2:17 But of the [tree of the knowledge of good and evil], thou shalt not eat of it: for in the day that thou eatest thereof thou shalt surely die.]
[tree of the knowledge of good and evil] = sight = os of abyssus

7:49:58 PM – I understand now I do not care about the sane or the ones with a sense of time which are the cursed ones or the neurotics. I am harming myself trying to communicate with something that has cursed sight. The sane have sight of hell. They sense time, that is a sight. They sense emotions. That is a sight. The sane bask in sorrow, anger, wrath, envy, gluttony, greed, pride. The sane are self defeating so there is no reason to cast stones at them. The sane are already cursed so there is no reason to attack them, they are being attacked mentally and physically by their self at all times. I will write my diaries and come to better understandings about this situation for myself but I certainly will never try to reason with rabidity. I show the sane compassion by being indifferent to them. I am not going to fight fire with fire I will show the fire it cannot harm me. - 7:54:43 PM

Mental world of the cursed = [Job 10:22 A land of darkness, as darkness itself; and of the shadow of death, without any order(unsound mind), and where the light is as darkness(blindness/false sight).]

[Psalms 23:4 Yea, though I walk through the valley of the shadow of death, I will fear no evil: for thou art with me; thy rod and thy staff they comfort me.] This comment is the Abraham and Isaac method, the those who lose their life will preserve it and submit.

Fear no evil = fear not. So one in the extreme left brain state after the education is in a situation of perceived death, a dark spooky place at night alone. Their hypothalamus is telling them the wind blowing is an evil ghost coming to kill them and they should run away but instead they [fear no evil]. Another example. Abraham is standing over one with a knife ready to drive it into ones heart and their hypothalamus tells them to run like the wind but instead they [fear no evil].

[shadow of death] is not actual death its perceived death. This comment is not suggesting if a Mac Truck is headed towards you to fear no evil it is saying if the shadow of a Mac truck is headed towards you fear no evil because it is a shadow, an illusion, a hallucination.

So this is an example that these ancient texts are saying the same thing over and over. Fear not, Fear no evil, Lose your (mental)life to preserve it, submit to perceived death. Face perceived death because after the education the perceived death is hallucinations and so once you face the perceived death the hallucinations stop. If one goes to a cemetery alone at night and keeps running away when they perceive death then they will continue to run away from perceived death because the Amygdala is the memory bank for fears caused by the Hypothalamus. On a shallow level, if one hears a cuss word is evil every time they think about using it and do not, they enforce that fear. Every time a person turns off music they perceive is evil, they enforce that fear of that perceived evil song.

Before one knows it they are a slave to these hallucination fears caused as a direct result the hypothalamus is giving them false positives or shadow positives of "danger". A person has a bad experience in the dark and so the memory is recorded in the Amygdala and every time that person is in the dark they are afraid and the hypothalamus keeps giving them this false fight or flight signal and this is all relative to the fact they have been conditioned so far to left brain from the education the parts of the brain that control fear are not working properly on a mental level.

The greatest fear of all fear is fear of death then there is fear of perceived death which is the same thing but, perceived death is relative to one's mind. A person can see a spider and run like their life depends on it but that spider may not kill them that person just perceives it will so in that case they ran from that spider because they believed it was actual death but really it was the shadow of death, or perceived death. A ghost will not kill anyone no matter how dark and scary the cemetery looks but if a person thinks some supernatural thing will kill them they are afraid of the shadow of death, perceived death, and so they should [Fear no evil].

So don't jump into a shark frenzy and then fear no evil because that is not the shadow of death, perceived death, that is actual death. I speak to a person who understands this mental self control conditioning. He told me scary movies do not scare him and he asked what else would work and the truth is, there are multitudes of locations where one would not want to go after dark, where the shadow of death lurks. Not literal death just the shadow, because if one has a sense of time which is a symptom of being in extreme left brain from the education, their hypothalamus will give false signals of death, the shadow of death at the first sound of a twig breaking in the right location. Once one understands what the tree of knowledge is literally and what the fear not suggestion by Abraham is relative to, these books are flawless in their descriptions of how to counter act the mental side effects of the tree of knowledge considering they were written thousands of years ago when there was no understanding of anatomy, psychology or neurology relative to today. These texts are written by people who read the text before it and then added their own take so they are interchangeable or they are all in sync.

[though I walk through the valley of the shadow(perceived) of death, I will fear no evil]
[though I walk through the valley of the shadow of death, I will fear not]
[though I walk through the valley of the shadow of death, lose your life to preserve it]
[though I walk through the valley of the shadow of death, submit]

This synchronization is a symptom of patterns and pattern detection is a trait of right brain. These patterns are all the same and easily detected but if right brain is veiled which it is as a result of 12 years of left brain education then they go unnoticed.

10:58:20 PM – I just had a death in the family. After baby blue died , she was a Catahoula leopard dog. I spoke of her in the third volume I recall perhaps the second. She had a heart tumor and we put her to sleep. We got lexie a black lab and we got both from the humane society and Lexie was a baby and was a stray and she had heart worms and that's why we put her to sleep or had her killed so she would no longer suffer.

Four years ago or so we had a dog Sugar and when she died I was very emotional and broken up about it for nearly two weeks and after baby Blue, five months after the accident, I cried for nearly an hour but this time I did not tear. I was right next to Lexie when they gave her an overdose of a sedative and I did not detect supernatural. One in the room with me was quite emotional and tearing and I understood what needless suffering was about. In the extreme left brain state emotions are turned up so high that one suffers.

Many beings have been killed or kill their self over nothing more than emotions and these strong emotions are a direct result of being conditioned into extreme left brain state as a result of the sequential heavy education. I am mindful we had Lexie killed because we were aware she was suffering in her condition and that is logical. The doctor suggested her prognosis for recovery was not well so we decided, and took care of the matter in about thirty minutes. That is logical. I am not capable of attachment but the details about that are simply in sound mind the time stamps are gone and so are the emotions so I have a picture of Lexie in my mind but no time stamps and no emotional attachment so I have no way to feel loss. We only had Lexie for seven months but my mind cannot tell what seven month is and my mind cannot tell what loss is. Lexie never insulted me and she never told me I was stupid because I could not spell the word cat properly.
Volume One - http://www.youtube.com/watch?v=gBYnhEkNod0 - 11:08:55 PM

[Genesis 19:25 And he overthrew those cities, and all the plain, and all the inhabitants of the cities, and that which grew upon the ground.]

[Genesis 19:29 And it came to pass, when God destroyed the cities of the plain, that God remembered Abraham, and sent Lot out of the midst of the overthrow, when he overthrew the cities in the which Lot dwelt.]

[Leviticus 26:31 And I will make your cities waste, and bring your sanctuaries unto desolation, and I will not smell the savour of your sweet odours.]

[Leviticus 26:33 And I will scatter you among the heathen, and will draw out a sword after you: and your land shall be desolate, and your cities waste.]

[Numbers 21:2 And Israel vowed a vow unto the LORD, and said, If thou wilt indeed deliver this people into my hand, then I will utterly destroy their cities.]

[Numbers 31:10 And they burnt all their cities wherein they dwelt, and all their goodly castles, with fire.]

[Deuteronomy 19:9 If thou shalt keep all these commandments to do them, which I command thee this day, to love the LORD thy God, and to walk ever in his ways; then shalt thou add three cities more for thee, beside these three:]

This comment relates to the education and the cities. Commandments relates to the remedy, fear not etc. As long as one applies the remedy, commandments, the education is fine and so are the cities. So this comment is compromise. Abraham just burned the cities to the ground and killed everyone in them.

[Genesis 19:25 And he overthrew those cities, and all the plain, and all the inhabitants of the cities, and that which grew upon the ground.]

But then this compromise happened where the cities and the education were acceptable as long as one kept the covenant or commandment which is one has to apply the remedy, fear not in order to avoid having an unsound mind. This of course is not what happened. No one applies the fear not remedy after the education. - 4:01:38 PM

10/27/2009 12:01:01 AM – [Matthew 24:15 When ye therefore shall see the [abomination of desolation], spoken of by Daniel the prophet, stand in the holy place, (whoso readeth, let him understand:)

Matthew 24:16 Then let them which be in Judaea flee into the mountains:]

[abomination of desolation] = [Leviticus 26:33 And I will scatter you among the heathen, and will draw out a sword after you: and [your land shall be desolate], and your cities waste.]
[your land shall be desolate] = Destruction of the environment because the species is essentially of unsound mind because of the extreme left brain state. Unsound mind means one is unable to live in harmony so their fruits or deeds are relative to their mind.

[[abomination] of desolation] = [Woe to the inhabiters of the earth and of the sea!] = [wolves.] = unsound minded = prone to violence = [double minded man] = [spirit of fear] = crescent moon mind, strong left brain veiled right brain = mentally [unstable in all his ways.] = [Galatians 4:10 Ye observe days, and months, and times, and years.] = emotional and have a sense of time = mentally cursed = [I will greatly multiply thy sorrow(*)]= [Genesis 3:14 And the LORD God said unto [the serpent], Because thou hast done this(got the education), thou art [[cursed(*)] above all cattle], and above every beast of the field; upon thy belly shalt thou go, and dust shalt thou eat all the days of thy life:]= [the serpent] = [1 John 2:18 Little children(lambs), it is the last time: and as ye have heard that antichrist(wolves) shall come, even now are there many [antichrists(wolves)]; whereby we know that it is the last time.] = materialistic based/ violent in their ways, [for the devil is come down unto you(you are of the beast)] = men of the tower] = [Genesis 11:5 And the LORD came down to see the city and the [tower](cities), which the children (the men condition their children with the education) of [men] builded.] = The sane = [They] = [beast] = [the dead] = emotional = [Galatians 4:10 Ye observe days, and months, and times, and years.] = emotional and have a sense of time = mentally cursed = [I will greatly multiply thy sorrow]= [Genesis 3:14 And the LORD God said unto [the serpent], Because thou hast done this(got the education), thou art [[cursed] above all cattle], and above every beast of the field; upon thy belly shalt thou go, and dust shalt thou eat all the days of thy life:]= [the serpent].

[2 Timothy 1:7 [For God hath not given us the [spirit of fear]]; but of power, and of love, and of a sound mind.]

[spirit of fear] = very emotional= If one is shy they are afraid. If one is embarrassed they are afraid. If one panics they are afraid. If one frets they are afraid. = [spirit of fear]

This spirit of fear is relative to the hypothalamus and Amygdala not functioning properly because the mind has been conditioned far too much to the left as a result of the many years of left brain sequential education. The disharmony which is relative to this [abomination of desolation] is all relative to having an unsound mind.

[spirit of fear] = [Revelation 19:20 And [the beast] was taken, and with him the false prophet that wrought miracles before him, with which [he deceived them that had received the mark of the beast, and them that worshipped his image.] These both were cast alive into a lake of fire burning with brimstone.]

[the beast]= [spirit of fear] relative to [For God(nature or normally?) hath not given us the [spirit of fear]].

[he deceived] them that had received the mark of the beast, and them that [worshipped his image.] = [Genesis 3:1 [Now the serpent was more subtil] = deceptive

[worshipped his [image.]] = [Genesis 3:6 ... [the tree was good for food, and that it was pleasant to the eyes, and a tree to be desired to make one wise,]..= Written language and math

[image.] = [it was pleasant to the eyes] = script looks good and is pleasing to the eyes.

[worshipped his image.] relative to when someone says "you misspelled that word so you are dumb" they are worshipping the image. They are defending the image. They are insulting a human being over an image or an inanimate object, a word.

It is along the lines of judging a human being on whether they respect the inanimate invention, "education" based on how well they learn it, and the more proficient they are at the "education" the further into left brain mindset they go. The more sequential left brain conditioning you get the bigger the reward you get and if you try to avoid the sequential left brain conditioning you get a slave job and are discriminated against by civilization.

"You are stupid because you didn't get enough sequential left brain conditioning so you get a slave job and are looked down upon by society and get a hard life"= punishment for not worshipping the image. The sane cannot grasp that because they would have to eat so much crow their strong ego would not allow it because they would have to understand this [Now the serpent was more subtil] really should be infinitely subtle. The sane cannot admit they have been infinitely suckered, deceived, tricked, the wool has been pulled over their eyes on such a huge scale their sequential simple minded thoughts cannot grasp such a complexity.

When an adult tells a child without an education you will have a tough life and have a tough job they know not what they do or say because they are really saying, If you conditioned your mind with this sequential conditioning you will be accepted in society and it will only cost you the complex aspect of your mind which is right brain. That is what the concept of selling your soul to the devil is relative to. Your right brain is your soul. It has complexity, intuition, heightened awareness, creativity, pattern detection , adaptability to the unknown or to change functions. Without that aspect you of the mind one is ruined as a being mentally, they have no soul.

So the reality is they sold their soul, right brain for a few copper pieces or the promise of a few copper pieces, money. They gave up their soul for some money or even the promise of money. Essentially they sold their soul; for an opportunity at luxury and they did it because the adults used fear tactics to encourage it. The adults judged them harshly when they resisted the education and in some cases even beat them or abused them to make sure they got the full measure of the education. Death itself is a welcome event in contrast to losing your soul, which is right brain, the unnamable powerhouse in your mind and thus your being and that is what "Give me liberty or give me death" is relative to.

There is only one choice in this world, I prefer to call hell. You either give up your soul, right brain, and have the potential for a luxurious existence without a soul or you resist and keep your soul but you are spit on by civilization, I call hell. Anyone who says anything contrary to that has already sold their soul for a few copper pieces. Once the right brain is veiled one is mentally dead, that is how powerful right brain is, and if one does not understand that it is expected because they are mentally dead. Slothful = sequential thoughts = mentally dead = an unviable creature, because their mental faculties are so diminished they are not able to function in situations of change, and situations that require complex concentration, pattern detection, adaptability. - 12:36:26 AM

3:23:03 PM – Intuition is a function of right brain. There are situations in life where intellectual knowledge which is knowledge gained by books will not suffice. These are spilt second intuition decisions and also decisions that are too complex to lay out and look for the answer in a book. There are too many situations one encounters in life with too many variables to expect the answer will be in a book somewhere.

One has to rely on their own intuition to determine what the proper way to deal with a situation is. After the many years of left brain sequential education the right brain intuition is nearly gone so this leaves a being in a situation they have to rely on what others say because they do not have the proper intuition abilities to make their own decisions. A sound mind, after one applies the remedy after getting the education, has equal power relative to intellectual knowledge, left brain, and intuition, right brain. This means both are combined so it is not actually intuition or intellectual knowledge it is someone in between those two that one relies upon to make decisions. Many of the sane try to look at past decisions to make current decisions because they have very little intuition ability and what this means is they are living in the past. They rely upon past decisions to determine future decisions because they have very little intuition and they also cannot mentally handle change.

Change is an unknown. Change can be scary. The sane are afraid of a bad haircut so instead of facing the unknown, change, they hold on to what is known even if it is harmful to them. The sane would rather make a bad decision based on known variables than make a decision based on change or unknown variables.

The right brain has this pattern detection ability. This ability is what helps one deal with unknown situations. With that pattern detection ability veiled one can only slothfully adapt to change and because of this one avoids change. Some of the sane speak about the world is ever changing. The world has been doing the same thing it has been doing for 5000 years and that is veiling the right brain of children based on the assumption this sequential based education makes one wise and the world is getting better and better at doing it proficiently, mentally raping children. Nothing has changed because the mental rape of children is still going on. Nothing is different. The education system has not produced one wise human being in 5000 years but it has ruined billions of minds. The sane cannot grasp that reality because they perceive progress is based on luxury. The inventions of the sane are simply solutions to problems they have created so they are not doing anything but engaging in infinite vanity.

There are too many people. The environment is going ill. There is not enough food. There are not enough jobs. There are not enough forests. There is not enough wildlife. There are too many suicides. There are too many wars. There is too much violence. There is too much drug use. There are too many family troubles. There is too much ethnic troubles. Countries hate each other and hate their self and spouses hate each other, and friends hate each other.

The sane are not inventing anything but self destruction because they keep conditioning the next generation into an unsound state mind and then they will say the children these days are really out of control. The reality is the sand got mentally raped by their parents via the education and they are doing the same thing to their kids. It will take me infinite books to scratch the surface of how mentally unsound the sane are.

It will take me infinite books to fully explain the extent of the neurosis the sane are in. The sane are in such deep neurosis they actually sense time mentally. The sane are in such deep neurosis they believe fully mentally veiling their child's mind will make that child wise, and they do it because all of their friends and peers in neurosis are doing it. The ones who the sane mock do not mentally rape their children. They send their children to special school that fully understands the damaging effects of the education on the mind. These schools have been around for hundreds if not thousands of years and they have teachers who dedicate their life not to teaching the sequential based written language and math as much as teaching it properly so it does not veil the right brain. The education is secondary to preserving the mind or leaving the mind intact after the education. The sane are totally blind to this reality because they rather sell the soul of their child, right brain, for a chance at some copper pieces and so they will be accepted in the civilization, I call hell.

If a person cuts the tail off a fish that fish cannot swim and it no longer viable. If a person cuts the wings off a bird that bird cannot fly so it is no longer viable. Swimming and flying are required for these two animals be viable. Right brain is required for a human being to be viable and so education veils it and so whoever is responsible for that is torturing that person. If one pays money to a system that mentally veils right brain in children they are complicit in the torturing of children and they are also complicit in all the problems that result from that.

It is not important that the sane understand that because they will attempt to look for that information in a book because if they had right brain unveiled they would understand that naturally via intuition. A book may tell one what reality might be like but intuition tells one what reality is like. I am mindful what I suggest in spirit is beyond the ability of one with a sense of time to grasp because that suggests their right brain is veiled so they are unable to understand what I suggest. That is not an indication of that persons intelligence it is an indication their mind is veiled and they are mentally unsound and are in need of a remedy to establish mental viability again.

Unfortunately that remedy is the one thing in all the universe the sane are least likely to do because it involves facing fear of perceived death and they are chock full of fear. If one is afraid of a word they are mentally off the scale of fear in their head. One cannot be more afraid than if they are afraid of a sound. This is not a loud sound this can be a quiet soft sound but somehow if that sound is a certain sound they will beat the child, wash the child's mouth out with soap, smack the child, insult the child over a sound. There is only one personality in the universe that would in any way harm a child over a sound that child utters. It is not the sound of the word it is the nature of the one who fears the sound of the word. If civilization, I call hell, were to suggest the word blue was evil and bad and anyone who said was evil and bad, soon enough parents would be harming their children for saying the word blue. There was no such thing as the cuss words we have today, 2000 years ago so it was not a bad word but today children get punished and beat all the time for saying these cuss words.

[Genesis 3:11 And he said, [Who told thee that thou wast naked?] Hast thou eaten of the tree, whereof I commanded thee that thou shouldest not eat?]

[Who told thee that thou wast naked?] = Who told you to be afraid/ Who told you to harm your children for saying sound? I want to know who told you. I want you to spend the rest of your days answering that question. Who told you to be ashamed, afraid and embarrassed? I did not tell you, so who told you? Here is what happened to you.

[Genesis 3:13 And the LORD God said unto the woman, What is this that thou hast done? And the woman said, [The serpent beguiled me, and I did eat.]]

[The serpent beguiled me, and I did eat.] =- You got suckered by one thing and infinite things at the same time. You trusted things that got beguiled and they beguiled you as a child. You were beguiled by the beguiled. I would not tell you that if it was not true. - 4:14:11 PM

5:23:24 PM – I am not exactly getting the results I would like to be getting with my explanations so I must rethink my strategy.

You were kicked from #???? by VoN ([Take your meds], wait an hour then come back)=[Acts 2:15 [For these are not drunken, as ye suppose], seeing it is but the third hour of the day.]

'If one does not understand a person, one tends to regard him as a fool.'

Carl Jung = [Amos 5:10 They hate him that rebuketh in the gate, and they abhor him that speaketh uprightly]

I do not detect I said anything violent or hostile to them. I said something that relative to me was just common knowledge but relative to them it was beyond their ability to understand so they determined I was a fool because their ego in the extreme left brain state would not allow them to understand they were a fool.

[16:15] <ToddR> Greetings

[16:17] <VoN> Greetings, human

[16:18] <ToddR> perhaps the least human among the humans

[16:20] <ToddR> I am writing a lot about Abraham in the 11th book. He was truly wise in his determinations and I am pleased with his efforts

[16:20] <VoN> Abraham Grant? Yes, I agree

[16:22] <ToddR> Abraham and Lot made quite a team but they were up against something that is perhaps something much strong than man

[16:23] <VoN> Lot? Which lot? The one they made after they paved paradise and turned it into a parking lot?

[16:25] <ToddR> I find great humor they insulted the sane to such an extreme yet the sane continue to publish their texts for over 5000 years without even being aware of it

[16:25] <ToddR> some sort of massive inside joke

16:25] <VoN> Dude, the sane are passe, we are the antisane

[16:26] <VoN> We publish our texts over the IRC for 9,999 years

[16:28] <ToddR> They will sink the ship if they are not reached and that will sink all of us

[16:28] <ToddR> One might suggest they give us infinite job security

[16:29] <VoN> Who are "they"?

This is where it started to go bad. He asked a question and he was not ready for the answer. He was not ready for the answer because here is how he reacted when I gave him the answer

[17:18] * You were kicked by VoN (Take your meds, wait an hour then come back)

But what is interesting is you will notice the pack mentality.

[16:29] <ToddR> It requires strategic words to reach one who is in such extreme hallucinations they actually mentally sense time

[16:30] <ToddR> they love their demotic script because they believe it makes one wise and that's a hard argument to counter

[16:31] <ToddR> Genesis 3:6 [... and a tree to be desired to make one wise,]

[16:32] <ToddR> They are not exactly wise if they perceive time are they?
[16:41] <VoN> Dude
[16:41] <VoN> I mean, dude
[16:41] <VoN>   Who are "they"?
/06[16:41] * VoN slaps ToddR around a bit with a crybaby crocodile

He is pushing for me to tell him who they are, when I said the word "they". He is waiting for me to be like him. He thinks his definition or reality is my definition of reality. Relativity suggests no humans definition of reality is exactly the same as any other humans definition of reality. He wants me to insult someone he does not like. He wants 'they" to be anyone but him or those like him. So I explain who "they" are.

[16:41] <VoN> Hi Aga
[16:45] <ToddR> [their] = [men of the tower] = [Genesis 11:5 And the LORD came down to see the city and the [tower](cities), which the children (the men condition their children with the education) of [men] builded.] = The sane = [They] = [beast] = [the dead] = emotional = [Galatians 4:10 Ye observe days, and months, and times, and years.] = emotional and have a sense of time = mentally cursed = [I will greatly multiply thy sorrow]= [Genesis 3:14 And the LORD God said unto [the serpent],
[17:03] <VoN> Dude
[17:04] <VoN> Why have you forgotten to take your neds today?
[17:04] <VoN> Go take them
[17:04] <VoN> Then come back
[17:04] <VoN> meds, not neds

All I said was "they" are the ones with a sense of time [emotional and have a sense of time = mentally cursed]. He has a sense of time and emotions. He is unable to say that is weird or interesting or explain it further because - 'If one does not understand a person, one tends to regard him as a fool.' = [17:04] <VoN> Why have you forgotten to take your neds today?

165

This is a good example of elementary sequential logic. There is no complexity in left brain, complexity is right brain. This means left brain is simple, simple minded. One who is conditioned by the education achieve extreme left brain state and they are simple minded as a result. There is no other way to explain it because left brain is the opposite of right brain and right brain deals with complexity. This is why education when not applied by an expert on the effects the education has on the mind, makes one simpleminded not wise.

Nothing I have suggested should make one say I am on drugs. I have not threatened him or said I see aliens and space men. I am talking about sense of time and emotions being a symptom. I may not have said it properly relative to what he perceives is properly but his perception of properly is not absolute properly just properly relative to him or to those who tell him what is proper.

[17:05] <ToddR> I am writing books trying to convince myself written language and math are not sequential based as in abc's and arranging letters in proper sequence because if it is, simply left brain conditioning.

I am aware they are getting angry. The pack is starting to get nervous. I am attempting to make suggestions to continue to talk to them. I am trying to make it so they will not become angry and hostile. The problem with the pack mentality is each person in this simple minded state of mind adds their own two cents and this creates a hostility among the pack because the pack acts as a pack because they cannot think for their self.

[17:05] <mishehu> looks like to me that he was playing ad-libs

Now this person adds in their observation. I am not like them so I am stupid. 'looks like he was playing ad-libs". This being would not know complexity if it was tattoo on their forehead so they insult it. This is what the pack mentality is all about. These two people have only said two things to my comments.

[17:04] <VoN> Why have you forgotten to take your neds today?
[17:05] <mishehu> looks like to me that he was playing ad-libs

And this is what this means 'If one does not understand a person, one tends to regard him as a fool.' And what this means [Amos 5:10 They hate him that rebuketh in the gate, and they abhor him that speaketh uprightly].

They hate the fact I tell the truth and they are not even aware of the truth when they hear it. I am suggesting to them sense of time and emotions are a symptom and they both have emotions, sense of time and simple mindedness so they are simply the blind leading the blind.

I do not know who these people are and the chat room is not relevant either because this is consistent all across the board in all chat rooms essentially. If they had intuition at full power they would read what I say and be aware of who was saying it. You may not understand that last sentence but it is truth also.

/01[17:07] <ToddR> so after 12 years of written edcuation ones mind become very left brain dfominate and right brain is veiled so the midn is like a cresecent moon to the point ones sense time
/01[17:07] <ToddR> its quite a quest
[17:07] <mishehu> VoN: you have any idea what ToddR is talking about?
[17:07] <mishehu> sounds like he's just making up things to me
[17:07] <mishehu> heh

[17:07] <mishehu> sounds like he's just making up things to me

This comment suggests what I am suggesting is so complex relative to this person understanding I must be making it all up.
[17:07] <mishehu> heh

He is laughing at what I suggest and his friends are watching and so he is mocking what I suggest.

[17:08] <ToddR> yes perhaps it requires one far wiser than I to explain it properly, whoever picked me certainly made an error perhaps
[17:08] * Zap-W (~z@84.228.221.124) has joined #israel
[17:08] * Kipi sets mode: +l 72

[17:08] * FireWALLs sets mode: +l 72

[17:11] <ToddR> neurologically once one is conditioned into the extrem left brain mind their hypothalamus and amygdala stop functioning properly and they are prone to fear and shame and embarssment and thus mentally their mind is confused and they cannot concentrate but that is perhaps to complex for the sane to grasp

[17:14] <ToddR> if one wants to make a nice slave condition them as a child to be unable to concentrate and prone to fear tactics and its all down hill from there

[17:15] <ToddR> so if fear is a side effect of the conidtioning then the remedy is Genesis 15:1 After these things the word of the LORD came unto Abram in a vision, saying, [Fear not],

[17:16] <ToddR> so Abrahm figured out the remedy and was the first to ever suggest it

[17:16] <ToddR> quite clever he was

[17:17] <ToddR> thus the abrham and issac story, isaac didnt run when he saw that knife over his chest so he feared not

[17:18] <VoN> mishehu: As I said, he forgot to take his meds

[17:18] * Jerusalem sets mode: +o VoN

[17:18] * You were kicked by VoN (Take your meds, wait an hour then come back-)

The point of this conversation should show one why Abraham slaughtered all the cursed beings in the cities. It is not they were killed because they were hallucination world. They were killed because they put the children in hallucination world. I am mindful you perhaps assume all the people who were slaughtered in all the cities in the ancient texts were killed by some supernatural aspect. This battle is strictly between the ones with a sense of time and the ones without a sense of time. It the battle of the minds and it is 5000 years old, and these ancient texts are simply the comments of the ones with no sense of time recording their attempts to defeat the cursed ones with a sense of time. Since you have a sense of time I am pleased you keep these ancient text in publications because they are assisting me in understanding how to defeat you and that is a good example of how the cursed ones defeat their self. The sane are publishing battle plans that are 5000 years old that are assisting in understanding how to defeat them. If you do not understand that is absolute reality then you just go back into your little hole and stay out of my way because I eat for no reason, boy.

Life with a sense time is very short so one is always rushed. With no sense of time life is very long so one is relaxed, so sense of time causes impatience and thus missteps and thus suffering.

6:56:52 PM – This is relative to economics.

Economics relies on labor and labor means jobs. There is a cloudy area in labor because some jobs require physical labor and some require mental labor. The concept of labor is an invention of man to justify economics and thus a monetary system and also to justify taxation. This is an indication of things being invented to solve problems created by the initial invention.

Early man did not spend his whole day looking for food. Early man did not spend his whole day looking for shelter. Early man did not give part of his food he gathered to some other person who did not gather it with him, taxes.

The family unit at that time relied on itself. The family unit was very aware of cause and effect because they relied on their self. If they starved to death it was on them and if they had enough to eat it was on them. What this means is early man had to be very good at everything. Early man had to be a jack of all trades and that is relative to adaptation. This jack of all trades ideal is eliminated in a job dependant economic system.

In a labor market one has to specialize and this means they have to focus on doing one thing very good and in turn they become reliant on other specialized services. A doctor is not going to be as proficient as a farmer at growing food or as an artist at painting a picture or as a bus boy at bussing tables.

A bus boy is not going to be very good at physics or at psychology as a physicist or a psychologist. This is not relative to intelligence or wisdom this is relative to specialized jobs caused by economics. Any human being can become a brain surgeon if the proper carrot and stick tactics are used. A human being will learn very quickly if the proper punishments are employs for not learning quickly. If someone says "I will reward you handsomely with lots of money if you learn this trade." that may be enough to encourage that person to learn that trade. All jobs are based on memorization. All jobs are based on repetitive tasks.

A surgeon is specialized in one area of surgery and they do that one type of surgery over and over with some variations but essential it's a repetitive task. A musical artist does the same thing over and over with some slight variations or adjustments to the patterns of the music they create. So a job is just repetition and one who does best is the one who can repeat that job most effectively and efficiently. Radiologists brag about how many X-rays or CT scans they can read in an hour without getting sued for reading them incorrectly. A bus boy brags about how many tables he can bus in an hour without upsetting the customers and thus being left without a tip. A lawn boy brags about how fast he can mow the lawns on his list without having the customers complain about the lawn. The important reality here is all labor is relative to time.

X = time to do job

Y = reward for doing the job fast

Z = job loss

A = job creation

B = job security

X is relative to Z

X + Y = Z

That is the fundamental problem with labor and that also suggest labor itself is prone to cause problems. The faster one does the job (X) the more jobs they do so the more money they make (Y) and the faster they are left with nothing to do (Z). Taken out to the largest scale, the species, the civilization is based on jobs and we have to keep creating jobs. Job creation itself (A) is contrary to Y.

Y + Z = A

The faster one does the job (Y) the faster one is out of a job (Z) and the faster one needs and a new job (A). If your job is intangible you are set and if your job is tangible you are screwed.

If ones job is to take pictures and they get paid to do it they are set because one can take infinite pictures. If ones job is to build houses and the housing market tanks they are screwed.

If ones job is to cure cancer and a cure for cancer is found, they are screwed.

If one specializes in finding a cure for cancer and they find one why would they hurt their self by revealing the cure.

A worker is dropped off at a location to mow the lawn. The boss says "Call me when you are done and I will take you to the next location." The worker is paid by the hour. The boss wants the worker to work as fast as possible because the boss gets paid by the location done. The worker gets paid by the hour so he wants to take his time.

From the Bosses point of view: $X = Y$ and from the workers point of view $X = B$.

If the worker works as fast as he can he will work himself out of a job. If the Boss does the jobs to slow he will work himself out of profit.

The ultimate goal of an economic system is self defeating. An economic system is based on working as efficiently as possible to make the most profit so one is eventually out of a job.

C = profit
D = work available
E = efficiency
F = unemployment

$E = C$
$E + C = F$

A large company buys a small company makes it more efficient and many lose their jobs. On a world scale the country that has workers who do the most efficient work for the smallest amount of profit are the only ones that will be left with a job. What that means is economics comes down to one reality, slavery. A person is never getting paid for what they do they are getting paid based on what others get paid to do that same job. This is relative to the monetary system. The bankers determine how much the money is worth and so they also determine how much the labor is paid.

For this reason a boss will never pay an employee how much they are worth because that goes against efficiency (E). It is in the boss's best interest to pay his labor as little as possible but still keep the labor working. It is in the labors best interest to do as little as possible but still remain employed. Some will suggest they take pride in their work but what they really mean is they take pride in their slave job. There is no one on the planet who wants to work a job; they were just told one needs a job to be alive.

The tribes in the Amazon get enough food for the day and then they communicate with each other, they fellowship. It is not important what they communicate about the point is they go grab some food that is abundant in the forest and they do not have to be a slave to do it. Certainly they die like everyone else eventually, but they do not die a slave.

The sane will suggest these tribes live a hard life because the sane live a hard life. This is relative to the pack mentality of the sane. The sane determine since there are six billion who work in this manmade economic system it certainly must be the proper life or the proper way and since the tribes who number perhaps far under ten million live in the wild still they must be improper. The absolute reality is it is relative to the observer and relative to this: 'If one does not understand a person, one tends to regard him as a fool.' - <u>Carl Jung</u>

The sane have never lived in the wild so they cannot possibility understand what it is like to live in the wild and live free. The sane have freedom to pick which slave job they want to work so they can remain alive. One cannot make money without taking money from someone else. These tribes do not have money. One or the other has to be wiser. The tribes do not need money because money is used to buy food and food is all around them. The sane have to have jobs to buy food because the food has been eliminated from being easily accessible. The tribes hunt and gather and the sane have that option eliminated. Civilization cannot hunt and gather because they have destroyed all the things they use to hunt and gather. The reason for this is money. One day someone understood if they killed enough buffalo they could make a lot of money from their hides.

E + C = F

Efficiency + Profit = unemployment, and in this case extinction of the buffalo.

This is why the sane are not capable of saving the environment because the sane perceive money is what they need to survive and that means they need to kill the environment to make money.

A shrimp boat goes out and catches as much shrimp as they can with no regards to anything but of money. Efficiency + Profit = unemployment/ extinction.

The government tries to regulate the amount of shrimp but they care more about money not the shrimp. So a rich shrimper pays a politician to allow his shrimp boats to catch a few more million shrimp each year and that puts money in the Politicians pocket and eventually Efficiency + Profit = unemployment/extinction of shrimp.

Conservation itself is a joke because conservation comes down to money.

It costs too much money to clean up all the plastic in the ocean that all the wild birds are eating and in turn dying from. Plastic is such a great invention certainly there could be no wrongs in the plastic invention. I ponder if the inventors of plastic had the intuition to understand the colorful plastic floating in the water is very attractive to sea birds.

So the sane invent plastic and then there is unintended consequences that require money to solve and they cannot let go of money to correct their errors so they neglect their mistakes and suggest they were unforeseen problems. I am certainly one of their unforeseen problems they may not survive. The sane know not what they do because their right brain intuition is none existent. The sane think one move ahead. If everything looks logical one move ahead it certainly must be proper a million moves ahead.

That is what pinprick sequential logic gets one, mountains of problems where there should be flat ground. It is called self destruction. It is called the species is suicidal. It is called the species is it worst enemy because it created education and it forces it on everyone, makes them mentally hindered and then is not even aware of it. You have been publishing these ancient texts for 5000 years that clearly say that, but you are too wise to understand that is what they have been saying.

[Genesis 2:17 - But of the tree of the knowledge of good and evil, thou shalt not eat of it: for in the day that thou eatest thereof thou shalt surely die.] - 8:23:44 PM

Mohammed spoke about Adam because Adam was the first human being in history to discover what causes the curse and come up with a sort of remedy to the curse caused by written language/ demotic script, which teachings survived and were found.

[1 Timothy 5:8 But if any [provide not for his own], and [specially for those of his own house], he hath denied the faith, and [is worse than an infidel.]]

[provide not for his own] is in random access it should be [does not provide for his own.]

[provide not for his own] = after one get the education a person should assist anyone with the remedy so the person is not left in the extreme left brain state and with a veiled right brain.

[specially for those of his own house] = it is most important for a parent to assist their own children with the remedy after the education.

[is worse than an infidel.] = this relates to how powerful of a crime it is to give a person this education improperly, and leave them in this crippled mental state where they are very prone to fear, cannot concentrate and are hallucinating to such an extreme they sense time, fear words, fear music and are ashamed not only of their own body but also of their own thoughts.

Infidel means one without faith. Faith is relative to the curse. Does one have faith Adam was telling the truth when he said this sequential based education thought to make one wise and knowledgeable puts a curse on one mentally when they adhere to it or learn it?

The reason faith is required is because one gets the education when they are a child so they never even feel what a sound mind is like before they get conditioned all the way to left brain, so they never even feel sound mind. So they have no contrast so all they can do is have faith Adam was telling the truth and apply the remedy.

For example, I did not apply the remedy because I thought I was in extreme left brain. I accidentally applied fear not as the result of a suicide attempt. I perceived I would die if I did not call for help and I decided not to call for help, save my life, so I applied [Luke 17:33 ..; and whosoever shall lose his life shall preserve it.] I decided to let go of my life and it turns out I didn't die, so I submit when I saw the shadow of death, perceived death, so I unveiled right brain. The moment you start to think I am anything but an accident we go down the idolatry trail. If you hate me you idolize me and if you love me you idolize me so just leave it at an accident. I am saying it is an accident and there is no one who knows better than me relative to the accident. I would tell you if I intentionally meant to do this. I did not intentionally mean to do this. I was trying to do one thing and I ended up doing another thing and that is why it is an accident. - 10/28/2009 3:03:05 AM

10/29/2009 9:51:43 AM – Living well sometimes requires embracing uncertainty. The steepest path seldom has rest stops. Bursting bubbles requires a sharp pen. Drawing in the sand requires the right hand.

10/31/2009 1:38:21 PM – This is relative to the remedy.

[Luke 12:31 But rather seek ye the kingdom of God; and all these things shall be added unto you.]
[Zephaniah 2:3 Seek ye the LORD, all ye meek of the earth, which have wrought his judgment; seek righteousness, seek meekness: it may be ye shall be hid in the day of the LORD'S anger.]
These comments do not say idolize the wise beings or make holidays or money making opportunities out of the wise beings.. These comments do not say "Turn the wise beings into a money making opportunity." [But rather seek ye the kingdom of God] = apply the remedy. One does not have the ability to think clearly with an unsound mind so first they should apply the remedy.
Once one gets the education it is a given they are in the hallucination world and sense time and a fearful so that is a mute point. This is the bad news [all ye meek of the earth]. This is saying the meek among the ones with a sense of time, earth. Earth denotes worldly which is material focused as opposed to cerebrally focused.

175

The reason this comment is bad news is because only the meek are in a mental state to wake up.

The ones who love hallucination world will mock what I suggest but the ones who are meek, depressed, suicidal will at least ponder what I suggest because they are aware something is not right. The meek are mindful something is not right in the "world". One has to apply the remedy when they are ready to try a true reality and that is what meek is.

There are not going to be very many rich and wealthy people who apply this remedy because they love hallucination world. They find no fault with it because their heightened awareness is nearly gone and they do not even sense something is amiss. The meek, depressed and suicidal are ready to get out which means they are ready to wake up.

[seek meekness] means one is mentally blind to the reality they are in after they get the education. Avoid thinking about the remedy because one will talk their self out of it. One will try to use their sequential logic and talk their self out of it. This is why the meek are the only ones prone to apply the remedy. Meek means one does not think or question the remedy they just apply the remedy.

The first thing one will say about the remedy is it is unsafe so one is prone to talk their self out of it. This remedy isn't about jumping into a shark frenzy, this is an ancient mind trick to break the curse caused by the many years of sequential left brain education. This remedy is as old as recorded history itself. One might suggest the ones in history who have applied this remedy have gone on to become quite productive in their lives. This is not productive relative to the last 500 years this is productive relative to the recorded history of mankind. Everything is centered around their message in the recorded history of mankind.

Everything is compared to them. The wise beings who suggest this remedy are the benchmark of mankind. Mankind is not mankind without these wise beings because mankind is not mankind without these wise beings teachings of this remedy. You do not know anyone of importance in contrast to these wise beings who suggested this remedy although you may not be aware of it. These wise beings did not suggest this remedy so you would idolize them. These wise beings suggested this remedy so you would apply it.

These wise beings sacrificed their life to make sure this remedy was recorded and handed down. These wise being were tortured and butchered wholesale just so you would be able to hear the remedy. They understood many would not apply it because they were not meek. They understood only the meek would apply the remedy because only the meek were aware something was not right.

This remedy is easy to apply as long as one is not hallucinating out of their mind and afraid of a bad haircut. You just think a place near where you live that you would be afraid to go to after dark. Not a scary place where other humans are. Be safe as far as bring something to protect yourself from other humans if that occurs but that is it. One is not looking to die one is looking to trick this state of mind into dying so they can reveal their true state of mind, so they can be reborn.

Reborn denotes one must first die unto their self and self relates to this state of mind where one perceives time. This sense of time state of mind is not you and so you have to trick it into thinking you have died so it lets you go then all you are left with you. Only the depressed even consider this remedy which is why you are going to have to [seek meekness].

Find a place that you perceive is scary after dark like a cemetery and go there alone and when your mind tells you something is coming to get you submit and be meek and allow it. Make up your mind when you hear a branch break and your mind is saying "You should run like the wind" you are going to deny that suggestion and allow whatever is going to happen to happen.

You are going to experiment and see if you can [though I walk through the valley of the shadow(perceived) of death, I will fear no evil]. Be in a spirit of experimentation. Be indifferent to winning or failure. Don't get discouraged if you cannot accomplish, apply the remedy the first time out or even the 100th time out. Do the best you can based on your understanding of this remedy.

It is done. Tis well.
10/31/2009 1:55:50 PM